The Raids on Zeebrugge & Ostend 1918

The Raids on Zeebrugge & Ostend 1918

The Royal navy Attacks on the German
Occupied Belgian Coast During the First World War

Ostend and Zeebrugge

C. Sandford Terry

Zeebrugge Affair

Keble Howard

LEONAUR

The Raids on Zeebrugge & Ostend 1918
The Royal navy Attacks on the German Occupied Belgian Coast During the First World War
Ostend and Zeebrugge
by C. Sandford Terry
Zeebrugge Affair
by Keble Howard

First published under the titles
Ostend and Zeebrugge
and
Zeebrugge Affair

Leonaur is an imprint of Oakpast Ltd

Copyright in this form © 2016 Oakpast Ltd

ISBN: 978-1-78282-557-9 (hardcover)
ISBN: 978-1-78282-558-6 (softcover)

http://www.leonaur.com

Publisher's Notes

Contents

Ostend and Zeebrugge

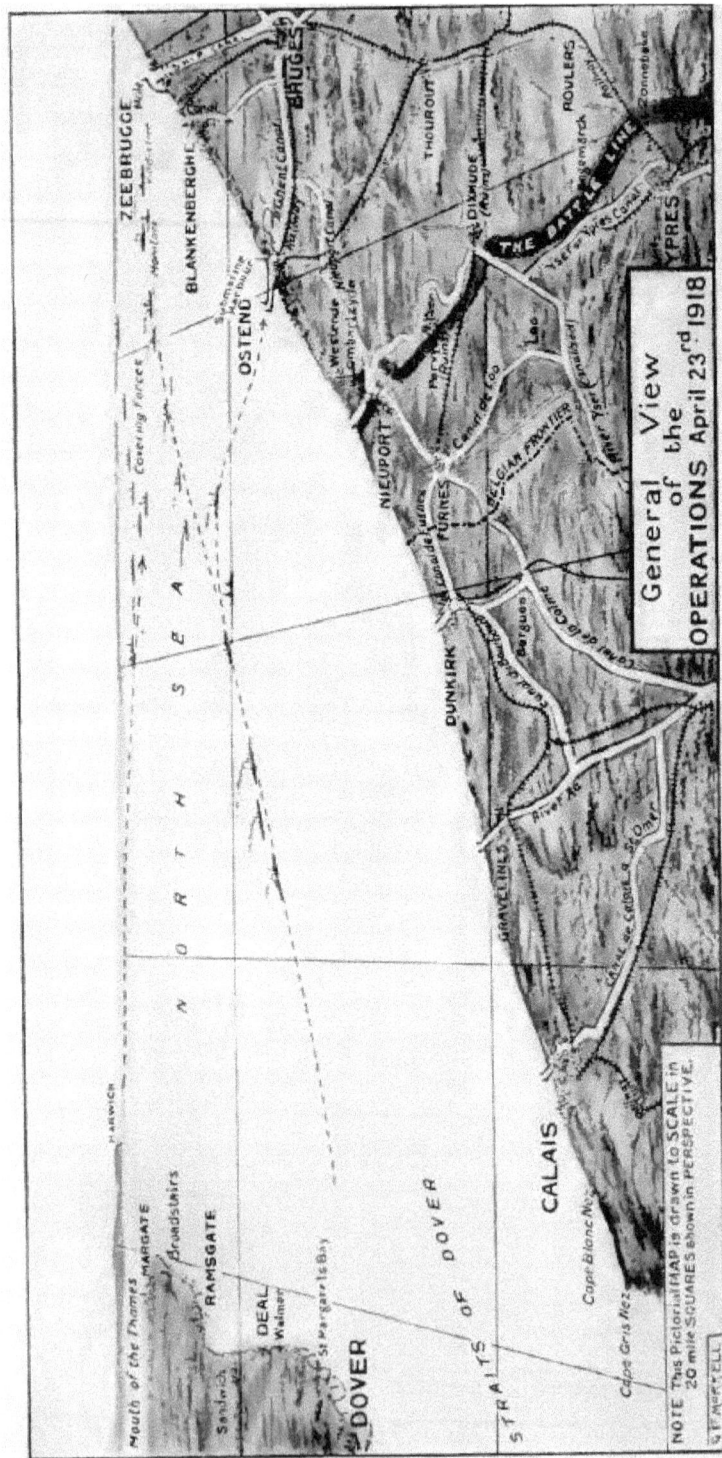

General View
of the
OPERATIONS April 23rd 1918

THE BATTLE LINE

NORTH SEA

STRAITS OF DOVER

Mouth of the Thames
HARWICH
MARGATE
Broadstairs
RAMSGATE
DEAL
Walmer
Sandwich
St Margaret's Bay
DOVER
CALAIS
Cape Blanc Nez
Cape Gris Nez

ZEEBRUGGE
BLANKENBERGHE
OSTEND
Covering Forces
Submarine barrier
Westende
Lombartzyde
NIEUPORT
Oude Veurne
FURNES
BELGIAN FRONTIER
DUNKIRK
Bergues
GRAVELINES
River Aa
Canal de Bergues
Canal de la Colme
Canal de Calais
50 ml

BRUGES
THOUROUT
ROULERS
Staden
Connebeke
YPRES
DIXMUDE
Yser or Yser Canal
Albert Canal
Ghent Canal
Antwerp
Passchendaele
Canal de Loo
Loo
Poperinghe
River Yser (Belgian)
Wesmacappelle

NOTE This Pictorial MAP is drawn to SCALE in 20 mile SQUARES shown in PERSPECTIVE.

G.F.MORRELL

NOTE.—The Harwich covering force actually was far distant, off the Dutch coast. The small craft detailed for action against Ostend proceeded from Dunkirk.

Contents

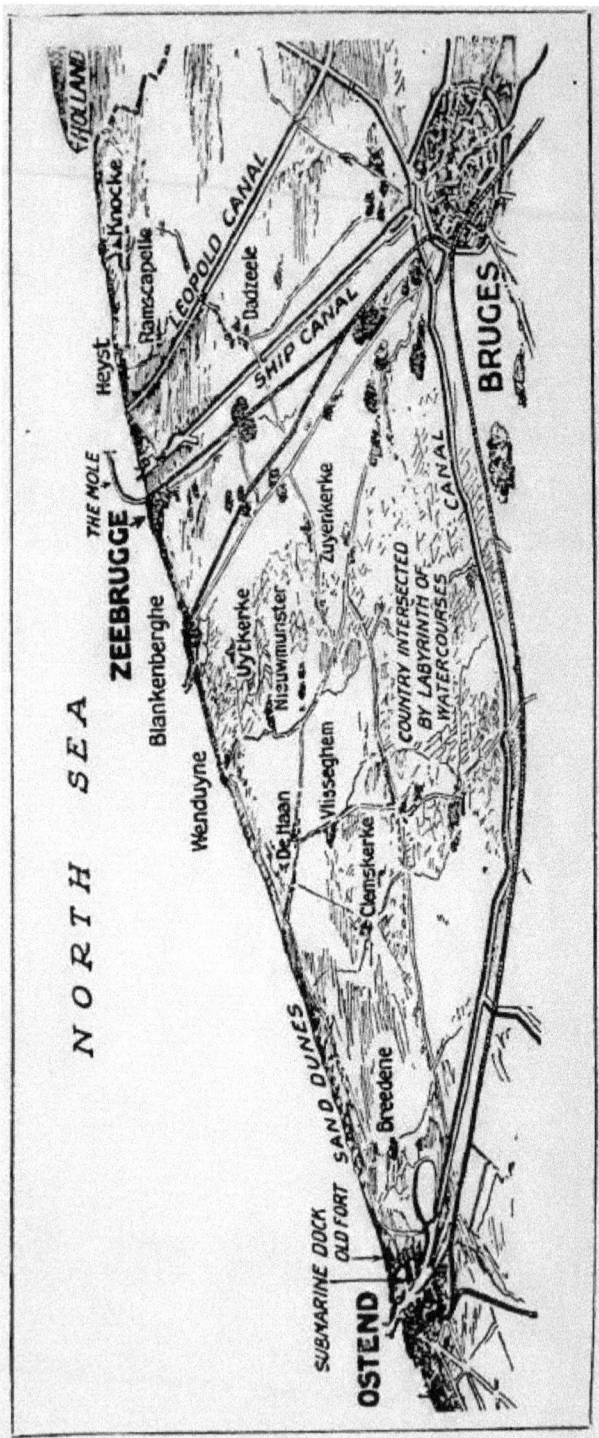

The Ostend–Bruges–Zeebrugge Canal System

CHAPTER 1

The Occasion and the Plan

On October 13, 1914, the unstemmed advance of the Germans forced the Belgian Government to evacuate Ostend. The enemy, already established in Zeebrugge, entered forthwith and remained in possession of the port until October 17, 1918. 'From either the naval or the military point of view,' *The Times* of October 17, 1914, announced with ill-founded optimism, 'the German occupation of Ostend is of no more account than the German band which played in the square at Bruges on Thursday night.' In fact, possession of the Ostend-Bruges-Zeebrugge canal system gave the enemy control of a stretch of coast outside his 'wet triangle', the Bight of Heligoland, which provided, in Bruges, an invaluable and protected base for the submarine offensive on which he relied to neutralise Great Britain's superiority in surface craft.

Both Zeebrugge and Ostend are connected with Bruges by canal, and Bruges itself with Germany by rail. Submarines could be dispatched in parts overland, be put together at Bruges, and find their way into the southern waters of the North Sea through the canals connecting their inland depot and the coast. At a bound the U-boat bases were advanced 300 miles nearer to the British lines of communication with the Continent.

The Zeebrugge-Bruges-Ostend system forms a triangle with two sea entrances. The eastern side is the canal from Zeebrugge to Bruges, and is eight miles long. The southern side, the smaller canals from Bruges to Ostend, is eleven miles long. The base, facing north-west, is the twelve miles of strongly fortified coast between Ostend and Zeebrugge. (Sir Roger Keyes's Dispatch of May 9, General Summary, para. 4).

No time was lost by Germany in developing her acquisition. Artillery of heavy calibre was mounted on the coast between Nieuport and the Dutch frontier. Between Zeebrugge and Ostend alone at least 120 big guns were concentrated, in addition to batteries of smaller ordnance for dealing with inshore raids. (Percival Hislam, *How we Twisted the Dragon's Tail*). As Lord Jellicoe remarked in August 1917, the Germans applied to this length of sand-fringed coast the principle of intensive fortification already adopted higher up the North Sea and on the island of Heligoland, and studded it with heavy pieces, in themselves infinitesimal targets at a range of more than 20,000 yards, on which a bombardment needed to be carried out.

★★★★★★

Between the Dutch frontier and the German right flank fronting Nieuport 225 guns were in position, 136 of which were of from 6-inch to 15-inch calibre. The latter ranged up to 42,000 yards (21 miles).—Sir Roger Keyes's Dispatch of May 9, General Summary, para. 4.

★★★★★★

That ships cannot engage land forts successfully is an axiom of naval warfare; the fortified Ostend-Bruges-Zeebrugge system rested seemingly secure behind the disqualification. While the ports served as lairs for destroyers and submarines, the country behind them was soon planted with aerodromes, whence with facility London and other cities became targets for German aircraft. Britain's insularity was doubly challenged.

Of the two ports Zeebrugge offered the greater utility to the enemy. It was more distant from challenging patrols on the Thames estuary and at Dunkirk, more difficult to approach, and, by reason of its protecting Mole, more difficult to attack. Its canal permitted the passage of destroyers and submarines of greater draught from Bruges to the sea. The Germans therefore concentrated their chief care upon it, equipped it with seaplane sheds, ammunition and store depots, floating docks and armoured shelters for submarines, and made it the principal outlet for their submarine, surface, and aerial operations in the lower waters of the North Sea. Ostend, on the other hand, lacking the protection of a defensive Mole, lying within range of the 15-inch batteries of the Royal Marine Artillery in Flanders, and connected with Bruges by canals inadequate to carry vessels of heavy draught, was subsidiary to its eastern neighbour. Originally a destroyer and submarine base, continuous bombardment caused the enemy to transfer its plant, docks (except one), &c., to Bruges. Ostend remained merely an emergency harbour for mosquito craft in difficulties.

While the Germans employed their ports at Kiel and in the Bight—Wilhelmshaven, Emden, Bremerhaven, Brunsbüttel, and Heligoland itself—as the bases for their Atlantic and distant operations, they proceeded to equip the Flemish ports expeditiously for a more localized service. Before the end of October 1914 Antwerp's shipbuilding yards were appropriated and skilled German workmen were introduced. Sections of small submarines dispatched by rail were assembled there, the completed vessels passing by canal to Bruges. By the end of November, six weeks after the occupation of Ostend, Zeebrugge had become an effective base of operations.

In the same period surface torpedo-craft or outpost-vessels, small and of indifferent quality, were built at Antwerp and sent through the canals to the coast. Two of them—A2 and A6—were sunk at sea by British destroyers on May 1, 1915. More powerful craft soon began to operate from the Belgian ports. Vessels of 1,000 tons displacement and 35 knots speed armed with three 4-1-inch guns made their appearance, (*How we Twisted the Dragon's Tail*), and on the night of October 26, 1916, ten German destroyers penetrated into the Channel for the first time, sank the empty transport *Queen* and the destroyer *Nubian* and disabled the destroyer *Flirt*. In April 1918 Bruges provided a base for at least thirty-five torpedo craft and about thirty submarines. (Sir Roger Keyes's Dispatch of May 9, General Summary, para. 5).

Standing, as they did, in dangerous proximity to our vital communications, military and economic, it became a matter of urgency either to recover the Belgian ports from the enemy or to prevent his intensive fortification of them. Rear-Admiral the Hon. Horace Hood, who was sent to Dover in October 1914 to organise a naval force as a prolongation of the retreating left wing of the Allies in Flanders, was not provided with the equipment for an adequate offensive. His successor, Vice-Admiral Sir Reginald Bacon, who succeeded him in command of the Dover Patrol in April 1915, also was limited to exclusively naval materials and to attempting by intermittent bombardments results unattainable completely by their means.

Theory and experience alike prescribed that, to achieve success, naval and military power should co-operate on such an enterprise as the reduction of the Belgian ports. (See Mr. Archibald Kurd's article, 'Zeebrugge and Ostend—and After', in the *Fortnightly Review* for June 1918.

Admiral Togo's failure to block Port Arthur and place the Russian

Fleet out of action in February–May 1904 provided a classic example of the axiom. But in and after 1914 the military situation made a co-operative expedition impossible. On the earliest stroke of war, the British Army, 'contemptible' in numbers but indomitable in efficiency and bearing, was called on to participate in the defence of France's soil against the invader. The interests of the whole Alliance, and not merely France herself, demanded that the industrial areas of France and Belgium and their populations should be rescued from the enemy before the battle-line settled down to equilibrium.

At the same time Britain was deeply pledged to protect Belgium and her neutrality. To regain her lost seaports was not less an urgent duty because it was prescribed imperatively by our own maritime interests. But the military forces the operation called for were needed elsewhere. In 1915, in addition to the Western front, Egypt, Gallipoli, and Mesopotamia made heavy calls upon the British armies. In 1916 Germany's formidable but fruitless attacks upon Verdun pinned them to the Somme and the Ancre. The Russian Revolution, which began in March 1917 and preluded the collapse of our Eastern ally, set free a vast number of German and Austrian troops, and threatened to give the Central Powers at length a decision on the Western front. If plans for a joint operation against the Belgian ports were formed, they were perforce abandoned. It behoved the navy to act alone.

The need for action was intensified by Germany's inauguration of unrestricted submarine warfare on February 1, 1917. Its heavy toll upon British, Allied, and neutral shipping, from its inception until the eve of the Zeebrugge-Ostend operations in April 1918, is exhibited in the following table.

Period.	Total.	
	Month.	Quarter.
1917		
February	574,856	
March	634,685	1,209,541
April	893,877	
May	630,336	
June	712,721	2,236,934
July	575,949	
August	549,363	
September	369,161	1,494,473
October	487,337	
November	333,443	
December	452,063	1,272,843
1918		
January	354,715	
February	388,542	
March	399,473	1,142,730

14

★★★★★★

See *The Times*, April 25 and May 23, 1918. The Table gives the gross tonnage of losses in the mercantile marine by mine and submarine.

★★★★★★

Dissatisfaction with the Admiralty grew as the need for more adventurous methods of combating the submarines was suspected. In November 1916 Admiral Sir John Jellicoe was summoned from the command of the Grand Fleet to succeed Admiral Sir Henry Jackson as First Sea Lord. The Naval War Staff was invigorated by the influx of younger officers with war experience, and towards the end of 1917 an inter-Allied Naval Council was formed for the 'co-ordination of effort at sea as well as the development of all scientific operations connected with the conduct of the war'. The adhesion of the United States to the Allied cause made a considerable accession of force available for naval operations and encouraged a more energetic prosecution of offensive warfare.

In November 1916 a proposal, made by Rear-Admiral Tyrwhitt, for the blocking of Zeebrugge was rejected by the Board. But twelve months later the Plans Division, of which Rear-Admiral Roger Keyes was the first director, had under consideration the blocking of both the Belgian ports. In November 1917 a plan of attack was prepared and reported to the First Sea Lord early in December. The objections which had overruled the proposal in 1916 were, firstly, the risk involved to the personnel; secondly, the contention that it was foolish to block ports into whose occupation we might ourselves hope to enter later. To the former it could be answered that the sacrifice involved in the operation was not greater than that incurred normally by the land forces of the Crown. As to the second, it was hardly doubtful that, whenever and by whatever agency he was ejected from them, the enemy would block and destroy the ports before evacuation. To leave him undisturbed in their possession until he saw fit to render them useless was a counsel of despair. These arguments prevailed, and, after Lord Jellicoe left the Admiralty (December 24), a conclusive decision was taken to put the scheme of the Plans Division into execution.

Rear-Admiral Keyes, as Chief of Staff in the Eastern Mediterranean Squadron in 1915, had been chiefly responsible for co-ordinating naval and military effort in the Gallipoli undertaking. It was doubly fitting, therefore, that on January 1, 1918, he should succeed Vice-Admiral Bacon in command (acting Vice-Admiral) of the Dover Patrol, commissioned to execute his own daring project. He proceeded at once to get together a staff to work out its details, to prepare the material, train the personnel, and fit out the ships the operation required.

★★★★★★

Among the officers killed on April 23 were many who shared with Sir Roger Keyes the secrets of the plan and the burden of its preparation. See their names in his Dispatch of May 9, General Summary, para. 30.

★★★★★★

The difficult problem for solution was, how to block Zeebrugge and Ostend, the doors of Germany's Belgian submarine system, without the co-operation of land forces, and with regard to the fact that each port had been converted into an exceedingly powerful fortress. It is a naval axiom that ships cannot successfully attack land forts: the ship, visible itself, fights an invisible target, and provides an unsteady platform for howitzers, to whose plunging fire land forts are particularly vulnerable. Nevertheless, Admiral Keyes proposed simultaneously to block two harbours defended by batteries of the heaviest calibre. Other obstacles were hardly less formidable. Among them was the difficulty of access. The Belgian coast is dangerous, beset by shoals, its navigation treacherous. Yet it was imperative to handicap the enemy's batteries by approaching them under cover of darkness, deprived of lights, marks, and beacons. The risks were great; any deviation from the proper course could not fail to lead to disaster. There was the hazard of mines, submarines, surface attack, and the risk of unfavourable weather conditions arising at a moment when it was too late to withdraw. (See an article by Mr. L. Cope Cornford, 'A Great Feat of Arms', in the *National Review* for June 1918).

Moreover, as seven hours' steaming at ten knots was required to bring the forces from their rendezvous of concentration to Ostend and Zeebrugge, sixty-three miles distant, at least four hours of daylight had to be encountered, during which enemy observation might detect and circumvent the operations. (Sir Roger Keyes's Dispatch of May 9, General Summary, para. 15).

In solving the problem, how to get the blocking ships into effective position, Sir Roger Keyes established a new precedent in naval tactics. Zeebrugge and Ostend canals being comparatively narrow, there was a good prospect of blocking them if the ships could be taken in. At Zeebrugge, on April 23, the intention was realised, one of the sunken ships touching both banks of the canal channel, and the other so nearly

BLOCK-SHIPS JOINING VICE-ADMIRAL'S FLAG OFF GOODWIN SANDS

achieving that result as to make it difficult to dredge on the open side without damaging the bank. At Ostend, on May 10, the prospect was not realised only because *Vindictive* was unable to fulfil completely the plans laid down for her.

★★★★★★

The statement, that *Vindictive's* failure was due to her draught being too large for the channel, is not accurate. The true reason is revealed in Sir Roger Keyes's Dispatch of June 15, para. 11).

★★★★★★

To sink a ship in the exact position marked out for her is a difficult operation. Unless the vessel sinks on an even keel, that end of her which drops first is carried downstream while the other end projects from the surface. Hence, instead of sinking athwart the channel, the vessel inevitably will lie along it, her width and not her length presenting an obstruction. The difficulty can be overcome by anchoring stem and stern before opening the main inlet valve. But at Zeebrugge and Ostend so slow a process was impracticable. Nor, in view of the strong current, could it promise to be effectual. The alternative was to secure that the ship should sink on an even keel by blowing out her bottom from end to end. To the efficiency of the device to secure that result the success of the Zeebrugge adventure is in great measure attributable.

★★★★★★

I follow here an exceedingly informing article, 'The Raids on Zeebrugge and Ostend', by Staff-Paymaster Cyril Cox, R.N.V.R., in the *Nineteenth Century and After* for June 1918. His conclusions are supported by a valuable array of historical examples. The block-ships carried on their bottoms mines fired by a time-fuse.

★★★★★★

The scheme established another innovation in naval warfare. It proposed to blind the enemy's heavy batteries by the use of a thick fog-screen, under cover of which the block-ships could approach their objectives. The employment of a smoke-screen was not a novelty in naval warfare. Von Hipper used it for the first time in the Dogger Bank action on January 24, 1915. The German High Sea Fleet used it in the later stages of the Battle of Jutland on May 31, 1916, to escape from Sir John Jellicoe's superior Battle Fleet. It was also in general use as a protective device against the attacks of underwater craft. But as cover for an offensive its employment was a novelty devised by Wing-

18

Commander Brock, R.N.A.S., 'a high development of the scientific use of smoke or fog—it is more fog than smoke—so as to protect the operation from batteries which could have flanked it,' and sunk the block-ships while still distant. (Quotation is from the speech of the First Lord to the House of Commons on April 24 announcing the Raid and its success. See Dispatch of May 9, para. 37).

At both Zeebrugge and Ostend, and particularly the former, the plan of assault involved the intricate combination of various classes of naval units and called for the concurrence of favourable physical conditions. No less than seventy-five vessels were engaged in the raid on Zeebrugge and over sixty in the simultaneous attack on Ostend on April 23, the success of the operation depending absolutely upon their nicest attention to a pre-arranged time-table—motor craft ahead to lay the fog-screen; vessels carrying landing- and demolition-parties to clear the Mole in advance of the block-ships; a submarine assault upon the viaduct to prevent reinforcement of the German parties on the Mole; destroyers in attendance upon monitors and in-shore ships to ensure them against attack from the sea; the block-ships themselves, the centre of this elaborate machinery; motor craft to take off the crews of the sunken vessels and to deal with enemy destroyers in the harbour; and off the Dutch coast, one hundred miles to the northward, a portion of the Harwich Force, under Sir Reginald Tyrwhitt, to hold at bay any intruders from enemy bases in Heligoland Bight; monitors and their 15-inch guns to engage the shore batteries; and overhead the aeroplanes—an extraordinarily complex mechanism whose efficiency depended upon each unit's meticulous fulfilment of its appointed part in the scheme.

While it was requisite that the operation should be nicely timed to take advantage of high tide, and yet avoid being caught by morning light, it was equally imperative, since the distance to be travelled on April 22-3 was about 100 miles each way, that the sea should be calm for the small craft. (The point of assembling or concentration, as has been stated already, was 63 miles from the Belgian ports, from Dover the distance is as stated above).

Also an on-shore wind was necessary to carry the covering fog-screen before the advancing vessels. Absence of fog was essential; a haze would be beneficial. These desiderata postulated a concurrence of favourable conditions. Even on April 23, at the third attempt to execute the plan, they were not all present; high visibility and, at the eleventh hour, a change of wind threatened to jeopardize the scheme

19

and rob it of success. On the other hand, better conditions had not occurred since the preparations were completed, nor did they recur within the period in which the operations were practicable. (Sir Roger Keyes's Dispatch of May 9, General Summary, para. 16, 18).

The project was both desperate and unique. A high naval authority, Admiral P. H. Colomb, (*Fortnightly Review*, June 1918), declares:

> Attacks on territory by the fleet alone, except by way of set bombardments for merely punitive or destructive purposes, are not now, any more than they were two hundred years ago, the proper objects for a navy alone to carry out.

Staff-Paymaster Cyril Cox, R.N.V.R., (*Nineteenth Century and After*), writes:

> Whatever place in the pages of history may eventually be accorded to the naval raids on Zeebrugge and Ostend, it is certain that no adequate parallel to them can be found in the records of our own or any other navy.

Various incidents have been recalled, but they accentuate characteristics that make the Raid of St. George's Day unique rather than furnish precedents for its ingenuity and daring.

In 1794 a combined expedition under Vice-Admiral Sir John Jervis and General Sir Charles Grey attacked Martinique, whose possession of the best harbour in the eastern Caribbean Sea made its acquisition desirable. As in the raid on Zeebrugge, the harbour was protected by a sheltering sea-wall. Otherwise, apart from the daredevil courage which marked both operations, there is little in common between them. H.M.S. *Asia* failed to breach the sea-wall inside the harbour and open a way to a party of bluejackets waiting outside in the bay to storm the citadel. Thereupon Captain Robert Faulkner, of the sloop *Zebra*, laid his ship alongside the sea-wall, scaled the parapet, and stormed the citadel. *(Nineteenth Century and After)*.

Two years later (1796) Captain Drury proposed to bottle up the Dutch fleet inside the Zuider Zee and put an end to its depredations upon British shipping. He planned to carry the batteries commanding the channel by means of landing parties, and, having opened it to the Fleet, to block the Texel with sunken Dutch merchantmen, re-embarking the landing parties when the Fleet had done its work, *(ibid)*. Save that the block-ships were to be provided from enemy vessels within the channel the project is not remote in conception from the Zeebrugge design. It was rejected by Admiral Duncan, and the fact emphasizes the boldness and confidence of the Admiralty in sanctioning at Zeebrugge a vastly more formidable risk. Three years later occurred the cutting out of *Hermione*.

An act of mutiny had placed the ship in Spanish hands two years before, in October 1799, she was discovered in the harbour of Puerto Cabello by Captain Edward Hamilton of H.M.S. *Surprise*. He resolved to cut her out from under the shore batteries. Sending six boats into the harbour under cover of darkness, he boarded *Hermione*, overpowered her crew, and in spite of a hot fire carried her out of the harbour. There are details of similarity to the Zeebrugge Raid, but as a deed of daring Captain Hamilton's achievement cannot rank with it. (*ibid*). Fitter to be associated with it is the expedition to Ostend under Captain Home Riggs Popham, R.N., in May 1798, which achieved the destruction of the canal gates. The landing parties, however, unable to re-embark, were forced to surrender. (See Popham's operations. *Journal of the United Service Institute*, Nov. 1918).

Recent history provides other episodes, among which the effort of Naval Constructor R. P. Hobson to sink the collier *Merrimac* in the fairway of the harbour of Santiago de Cuba is most familiar. The attempt was made on June 3, 1898. The Spanish Fleet under Admiral Cervera lay within the harbour. Admiral Sampson and the American Fleet waited outside. Under heavy fire Hobson succeeded in taking *Merrimac* into the harbour and sank her; but the harbour was not blocked, and the American Army eventually delivered the Spanish Fleet into Sampson's hands by capturing Santiago and forcing Cervera out to sea. (*Fortnightly Review*, June 1918; *Nineteenth Century*).

Equally indicative of the disadvantages under which naval power lies in an unsupported challenge to a defended enemy port is the familiar effort of Admiral Togo to destroy the Russian Fleet in Port Arthur in February-May 1904. Three attempts were made by the Japanese to block a channel too wide to be closed by a single ship. At the first attempt (February 23-4) three of the five ships sent in were sunk by Russian fire before they reached the harbour entrance; the other two sank themselves, but at some distance from the channel. A month later (March 26-7) the Japanese sank four ships, but ineffectually; the Russian Fleet came out to assert its continued liberty. Five weeks later (May 2-3) twelve ships were requisitioned for blocking purposes and eight of them were sunk; but the harbour was not effectually sealed. The circumstances demonstrate the destructive power of well-placed land batteries trained upon blocking-ships in a narrow channel. In sea-power the Japanese were superior to the Russians. Yet their unsupported naval measures failed to put the Russian Fleet out of action. (*Nineteenth Century; Fortnightly Review*).

The sinking of the collier *Newbridge* in the Suninga Channel of the Rufigi River in November 1914 was a small affair, but it illustrates the difficulties to be overcome in blocking a channel. The German cruiser *Königsberg* having been located there, it was resolved to close the river against her egress. Escorted by a small flotilla of ships' steam-boats, *Newbridge* steamed to the spot where it was decided to sink her, anchors were dropped at head and stern, the main valve was opened, and she began to settle. The crew stepped off into a waiting steam-cutter, fired the explosive charge, and withdrew.

★★★★★★

Nineteenth Century. Staff-Paymaster Cox remarks, as proving how difficult is the operation, that the Turks on several occasions tried to block the Shatt-al-Arab and Tigris to prevent our naval advance in Mesopotamia. Not once were they successful. The Germans were equally unsuccessful in their efforts to block the Cameroon River against our passage to Duala in the early stages of the West African campaign.

★★★★★★

A review of these imperfect parallels heightens appreciation of the Zeebrugge adventure as a superb effort of human courage. Had it failed the story of the nation still would have been richer for a great tradition. In fact, overcoming impediments of many kinds that threatened failure, it won triumph for a project audaciously conceived. Luck attended it, and deservedly. A plan so laboriously prepared, whose details in the last stages were shared by so many actors in it, might have leaked out. The necessary factor of surprise might have been sacrificed, and the enemy have been prepared to effect the destruction of the expedition before it reached its destination. A single scouting sea-plane or patrol boat would have deprived the adventure of the first condition of success. Neither was encountered. More serious still, a mine-field laid in an unexpected area might have destroyed the vessels before their task was accomplished. No foresight could prevent these contingencies from happening. They were challenged in a spirit of buoyant optimism, with a love of adventure for adventure's sake, that priceless disposition of the race, and with unswerving confidence in the mind that conceived and the hands that guided the operation.

CHAPTER 2

St. George's Day Raid, April 23, 1918

By the beginning of April, the projected attack on Zeebrugge and Ostend was planned to the last detail. The special ships the service demanded had been assembled and fitted at Chatham. Volunteer crews had been selected and trained for the particular operations in which they were to take part. To block the Zeebrugge section of the Bruges Ship Canal was the chief object. The concurrent closure of Ostend seemed necessary to complete the sealing-up of the waterways radiating from Bruges. Otherwise, lighter craft, denied an exit via Zeebrugge, would pass more or less freely through the smaller channels that debouch on the sea at Ostend.

A subordinate, but important, purpose was to inflict as much damage as possible on the harbour works and defences of the two ports. If successful, the operation promised to set back the enemy's submarine bases three hundred miles, which roughly is the distance from Zeebrugge to Emden, to seal-up his torpedo craft at Bruges, to free the Dover Patrol for service in the wider antisubmarine campaign, and to relieve our military and economic communications of an intolerable menace. (See Sir Roger Keyes's Dispatch of May 9, General Summary, para. 3; 'Zeebrügge', Mr. A. H. Pollen, *Land and Water*, May 2, 1918 and *The Navy in Battle*-1918).

The forces to which the operation was entrusted consisted of monitors armed with heavy guns to tackle the shore batteries; destroyers to provide a protecting cover to the ships detailed for the attacking operations; motor boats and launches to lay the smoke-screens, rescue the crews of the block-ships, and engage enemy destroyers and other craft that might be found in the harbours; five obsolescent light cruisers for use as block-ships, filled with cement and fitted with explosive charges and mines attached to their bottoms; a sixth light

23

cruiser, H.M.S. *Vindictive*, two Mersey ferry-boats, *Daffodil* and *Iris II*, and two obsolescent submarines, all detailed to attack the Mole at Zeebrugge and divert attention from the block-ships, the sinking of which in their appointed places was the main object to be achieved. The expedition, which numbered over one hundred and forty vessels of all kinds, was under the command of Vice-Admiral Roger Keyes in H.M.S. destroyer *Warwick*. Commodore Hubert Lynes directed the operations at Ostend.

★★★★★★

The numerous small craft detailed for the Ostend Raid were based on Dunkirk. The block-ships *Sirius* and *Brilliant* and two attendant destroyers alone made the passage from Dover with the Zeebrugge force.

★★★★★★

The Harwich Force, under Sir Reginald Tyrwhitt, cooperated off the coast of Holland in order to watch any movement by the enemy from the direction of Heligoland Bight. The Dover Wings of the Air Force and the guns of the Royal Marine Artillery in Flanders were warned to bombard the shore batteries, in order to obstruct their concentration on the block-ships. On several nights prior to April 22 a bombardment had been carried out. Consequently, the enemy had no reason to anticipate particular action on the night of the operation. (Dispatch of May 9, General Summary, para. 20).

There being two points of attack, the operation resolved itself into two distinct and simultaneous undertakings, the expedition breaking up into unequal portions to carry them out. In both cases the element of surprise was essential to success. Concealment was to be secured by smoke-screens laid by the small motor-craft steaming ahead. A daring rush into the teeth of the shore batteries, distracted by bombardment from sea and air, was relied on to carry the concrete-laden cruisers to their blocking positions within the canals.

At Ostend the operation was at once more simple and more diffi-cult. No protecting Mole covered the approach to the canal entrance, as at Zeebrugge. The problem was simply to run in *Sirius* and *Brilliant* from under the smoke-cover and place them between the harbour piers before the enemy could sink them elsewhere. The operation failed, partly through a change of wind at the last moment, chiefly be-cause the enemy had previously shifted the Stroom Bank buoy mark-ing the channel to the harbour a mile to the eastward. The concrete-laden cruisers, picking up the false guide, and putting their helms to starboard, consequently ran ashore. (Sir Roger Keyes's Dispatch of May 9, General Summary, para. 26).

At Zeebrugge the operation was complicated by the problem of the Mole on the west side of the harbour—that is, on the starboard side of the block-ships as they steamed towards the canal gates. The structure—used by the Germans as a supply, air, and destroyer base—is one and a half miles long by 100 yards wide. A battery of three 5-9's, and six smaller guns on the extension, guarded the entrance. Five hundred yards of viaduct connect the Mole with the shore, on which other batteries were planted for its protection. (The necessity to counteract the silting of the harbour explains why the Mole is broken by a viaduct which opens it to the sea for 500 yards).

At Zeebrugge, consequently, the block-ships were threatened both by shore batteries, as at Ostend, and also by the Mole batteries and machine-guns. It was especially necessary to put the battery at the sea end of the Mole out of action before the block-ships—*Thetis*, *Intrepid*, and *Iphigenia*—entered the harbour. (The attack on the Mole, conducted on such a scale as to suggest that it was the main operation, was shrewdly planned to conceal and also promote the real object of the expedition).

The task was entrusted to landing parties carried by the old cruiser *Vindictive* and the two ferry-boats *Iris* and *Daffodil*. To cut off the Germans on the Mole from reinforcement two submarines were detailed to blow up the iron viaduct connecting it with the shore. The submarine attack was entirely successful. *Vindictive* imperfectly fulfilled her commission. But without serious molestation from the Mole's defences the block-ships were able to steam the last mile of the course. Two of them—*Intrepid* and *Iphigenia*—sank themselves in the fairway of the canal and effectually bottled it up. Motor-launches rescued their heroic crews. The ferryboats *Iris* and *Daffodil*, being of large carrying capacity, double hulled, and practically unsinkable, were provided chiefly for the rescue of the landing parties in the event of *Vindictive* being sunk. (*Iris II* and *Daffodil* also carried landing parties).

A counterattack by the powerful Destroyer Flotilla inside the harbour was anticipated. In fact, the greater part of it had been withdrawn to Bruges. One destroyer emerged and is believed to have been torpedoed by a C.M.B. Others remained alongside the Mole and their crews took part in its defence. (Dispatch of May 9, General Summary, para. 10).

As has been remarked already, so complex a scheme demanded

the concurrence of favourable conditions of weather and atmosphere. Throughout April the crews of the block-ships, lying in the West Swin anchorage, debarred from communication with the shore, waited eagerly for their arrival. Twice the whole armada concentrated at sea, and once, on April 11-12, got to thirteen miles from Zeebrugge, when weather conditions compelled it to return.

★★★★★★

Of the two occasions mentioned in the text, once the weather compelled abandonment of the operation within an hour. See an interesting article by Lieut.-Commander E. Hilton Young, R.N.V.R., in the *Cornhill Magazine* for December 1918. The author was a Lieutenant R.N.V.R. on *Vindictive* on April 23. See the Dispatch of May 9, General Summary, para. 18).

★★★★★★

At length, on April 22, St. George's Eve, satisfactory conditions invited a third venture.

The considerable a
rmada converged upon the scene of action from four points.

★★★★★★

See Dispatch of May 9, para. 45 ff. Excluding the Harwich covering force (23 ships) and the parent ships (3) the striking force numbered 142 vessels (see Dispatch, para. 31). Of these, 75 were engaged at Zeebrugge and 67 at Ostend.

★★★★★★

A covering force of light cruisers and destroyers operated from Harwich towards the Dutch coast. In the West Swin, the main channel from the Nore to the north, the five block-ships, with *Vindictive*, *Daffodil*, and *Iris II*, awaited the summons. At Dunkirk the monitors (six), destroyers, M.L.s and C.M.B.s—in all forty-seven vessels, including nine French M.L.s and T.B.D.s—part of the force detailed for the Ostend operations, were assembled. At Dover the rest of the force was concentrated.

At 1.10 p.m. the Swin ships, and at 2.0 p.m. the Dover contingent, proceeded to join Sir Roger Keyes off the Goodwin Sands, and thence to a rendezvous 63 miles from their objectives; the speed was 10 knots, for the pace of the block-ships was slow. At 4. 53 p.m. the force set out from the rendezvous for its destination. It was disposed in three columns, Warwick, Phoebe, and North Star, detailed to cover *Vindictive* from torpedo attacks while the storming operations were in progress, forming the starboard column. Every craft was towing one or more C.M.B.s, and M.L.s steamed between the columns. The Ostend force proceeded thither from Dunkirk under the orders of Commodore Lynes.

★★★★★★

It was a brave and unusual array that swept to the north-east as the light faded from the sky. Modern destroyers steamed on the wings of the columns, one of which flew the flag of Vice-Admiral Roger Keyes, C.B., C.M.G., D.S.O., M.V.O., the old *Vindictive* in the van of the centre column with the *Iris* and *Daffodil* in tow, for all the world like veteran hound on the trail with her two puppies on her flanks; the five valiant block-ships followed, each with specially detailed parties below stoking for all they were worth, that their old ships' last voyage should be made at a seemly speed. A cloud of motor-launches filled the waterways between the columns, and the two obsolete sub-marines, with their escorting picket-boat, proceeded in tow of destroyers.—*The Navy Eternal* (1918), by 'Bartimeus'.

★★★★★★

The greater part of the passage of the main force having to be carried out in broad daylight, all the scouting planes of the Patrol were employed to detect the appearance of enemy craft. As the normal means of communication might put him on guard, the movements of the scattered forces were governed by a time-table, which was observed with extraordinary punctuality. Visual signals were reduced to the minimum of necessity; wireless signals (with one exception) were forbidden. Special aids to navigation were laid down in advance to guide the attacking force and the monitors to their positions.

On arrival at a certain position, the conditions continuing to be favourable, a prearranged wireless message was sent (8.45 p.m.) to the detached divisions in the north and at Dunkirk signifying that the programme would be adhered to. Fifteen miles or so from its objectives, the main force stopped at 9.55 p.m. to enable the surplus crews to be disembarked on to an attendant mine-sweeper, and to slip the C.M.B.s. At 10.30 p.m. *Sirius* and *Brilliant* and their escort of two destroyers proceeded towards Ostend. The rest went on to Zeebrugge.

The striking units detailed for the attack on Zeebrugge, (Dispatch of May 9, para. 56 ff.), were the three block-ships. *Vindictive* and her attendant ferry-boats, submarines C 1 and C 3, a flotilla of twenty-four M.L.s and eight C.M.B.s for laying smoke screens and rescue work, and nine C.M.B.s to attack vessels inside the Mole. Two monitors were stationed out to sea for long-range bombardment, but, owing to poor visibility and an unusual set of the tide, its opening was delayed somewhat beyond the time prescribed in the programme of operations, (*ibid*).

At 11.20 p.m. the monitors opened fire. At 11.40 p.m. the C.M.B.s, running in close, set up the necessary 'fog' and came under heavy fire during the operation. Almost simultaneously the wind died away, and, coming again from a southerly direction, lessened the effectiveness of the smoke-screen. At 11.56 p.m. *Vindictive*, with *Daffodil* and *Iris II* in her rear, passed through the 'fog' and found the end of the Mole's giant structure 300 yards distant on the port bow. At 12.1 a.m., one minute beyond her programme time, she was alongside. Three minutes elapsed before *Daffodil* arrived and pushed *Vindictive* to the Mole to enable the special anchors to hook the parapet. The heavy roll caused by a three-knot tide, and the scend alongside the Mole, prevented the ship from placing them and broke up the foremost of them. Most of the landing brows were broken by gunfire. The two foremost, however, reached the wall, and two others eventually were got into position. The storming and demolition parties poured over them and began a valiant assault upon the Mole's garrison and defences which is detailed elsewhere.

Daffodil arrived at 12.4 a.m., and throughout the operations was obliged to drive her stern against *Vindictive's* starboard side to hold her to the Mole. *Iris II* followed close and took station ahead of *Vindictive*. In her case also the scend of the sea and roll of the ship made it impossible to fasten the Mole anchors. *Iris* fell back behind *Vindictive*, and prepared to land her parties across the cruiser, but hardly had begun to do so when the withdrawal signal was sounded.

The programme allowed twenty-five minutes for carrying through the attack upon the battery of three 5.9-inch guns at the seaward end of the Mole, and for isolating the Mole from reinforcements by the destruction of the Viaduct. The latter task was achieved completely, the former imperfectly. Meanwhile, at 12.25 a.m., *Thetis*, leading the other two block-ships, passed the end of the Mole and made her way to the entrance of the Ship Canal. (Dispatch of May 9, para. 92 ff). The plan of operations had been the object of particularly close consideration. If *Intrepid* and *Iphigenia* were observed to be following her, *Thetis* was instructed to ram the lock-gates, while the other two sank themselves near the entrance at the southern end of the Canal piers, where, irrespective of the success or failure of *Thetis*, they would be certain to set up silt.

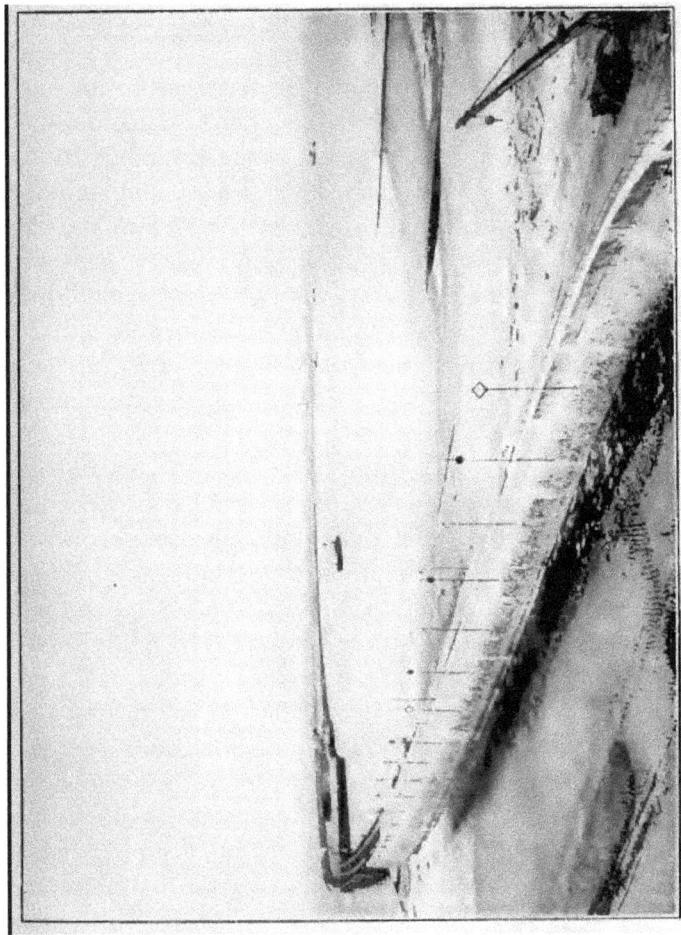

THE MOLE AT ZEEBRUGGE, GENERAL VIEW

Circumstances prevented *Thetis* from carrying out her instructions. Under fire from the Mole extension's six guns, but unmolested by the 5.9-in. battery, whose attention was diverted from the block-ships by the naval landing party, she made for what appeared to be an opening in the defensive obstruction in the harbour, fouled the nets, and was 300 yards from the eastern pier-head when both her engines were brought up. She had a list to starboard and was settling down, having been frequently holed on her Mole side by gun-fire. Her starboard engine was restarted, however; her head was swung into the dredged channel; the charges were fired, and the ship quickly sank. But she had cleared a path for her consorts. Her crew were taken off by M.L. 526.

Intrepid, directed by *Thetis*, passed her leader, and unmolested by enemy gun-fire—which was concentrated on *Thetis* and *Vindictive*—reached her assigned position in the canal, where she was sunk. All of her crew, with one exception, were got away, mainly through the heroism of M.L. 282, commanded by Lieutenant Percy T. Dean. R.N.V.R. (She had a complement of 87 instead of 54, her surplus crew had not been taken off, chiefly owing to their determination to take part in the fight. See the Dispatch, para. 95).

Iphigenia, last of the block-ships, twice hit on the starboard, or Mole, side, made for the gap which *Intrepid* had left between herself and the eastern bank of the Canal. With complete success her commander reached his position, fired the charges, and sank the ship. Her crew were rescued, with few casualties, by M.L. 282. Not the least detail of a hazardous adventure is the heroism of M.L.s 282 and 526. M.L. 110, their partner in the work of rescue, was sunk.

Besides their screening duties, the C.M.B.s were employed in attacking enemy vessels within the Mole's protection. Most of the German Flotilla had been withdrawn to Bruges before the action, and only two craft lay alongside the Mole, apparently without having steam up, (Dispatch of May 9, para. 10). C.M.B. 7 reported a torpedo hit upon one of them. C.M.B. 32 A fired a torpedo at Captain Fryatt's old ship *Brussels*, and an explosion followed, C.M.B. 5 encountered a destroyer emerging from the harbour and torpedoed her below her forward searchlight.

★★★★★★

Dispatch of May 9, para. 120. On October 14, 1918, the Brussels was again attacked as she lay alongside the store shed on the Mole. She was used as a torpedo training ship.

★★★★★★

The destroyer *North Star* also discharged her torpedoes at vessels alongside the Mole, but coming under very heavy fire at point-blank range was disabled and eventually sank, (Dispatch of May 9). Two motor-launches also were lost. The material casualties of the adventure were extraordinarily slight.

The attack on Zeebrugge was completely successful in achieving the first and most important object of the operations—the outlet of the Bruges Ship Canal to the sea was effectually blocked. The second object—the sealing of the entrance to Ostend harbour—was not achieved, for reasons which reflect in no way upon the plan or those responsible for its accomplishment.

Sirius and *Brilliant* were timed to reach the entrance to Ostend harbour at midnight, (*ibid*). At 11.20 p.m. the six monitors began their bombardment, (*ibid*). The smoke-screen craft performed their task successfully until, at 11.50 p.m., the wind changed to from off-shore. Ten minutes later the block-ships arrived at the Stroom Bank buoy, where they were to find their direction for the harbour. Arrived there, and meeting the adverse smoke, they were prevented from taking bearings which would have shown them that the buoy had been moved to a point 2,400 yards east of its accustomed situation. Taking a line which, had the buoy been in its original position, would have led them into Ostend harbour, the two block-ships drove ashore some 2,400 yards east of it, (*Ibid* , para. 26; Commodore Lynes's Report, para. 6a, 11d).

Brilliant, who was leading, observing breakers where the Ostend piers should have been seen, starboarded her helm, but too late to avoid grounding. *Sirius* put her helm hard over and her engines astern. But the ship, badly damaged by gun-fire and sinking, did not answer the helm, collided with the port quarter of *Brilliant*, and grounded firmly. Both were blown up where they stranded at 12.30 a.m. Their crews were rescued by M.L.s 276 and 283. A small party of *Sirius*'s crew pulled thirteen miles out to sea before they were picked up by *Attentive*. (Dispatch of May 9, para. 25, 98 ff.)

Meanwhile, at 1 a.m. the 'retirement' had been sounded. Until daylight the destroyers continued to cruise and pick up stragglers. No enemy craft were seen, and at 7.30 a.m. the force returned to Dunkirk. All the crews of the block-ships were saved. All the M.L.s returned intact, with very slight casualties. The C.M.B.s were equally fortunate, and their personnel casualties were only six wounded. But the operation, partly owing to the change of wind, chiefly to the success of the enemy's *ruse de guerre* in changing the situation of the Stroom Bank buoy, was a failure. (Commodore Lynes, para. 11–13). Ostend harbour remained open from the sea and for the passage of small craft through the lesser waterways from Bruges. The operations of May 10 were necessary and were already contemplated.

(A) Captain Carpenter's Narrative.

(*The Times*, April 26, 1918. Commander-now Captain-Alfred Francis Blakeney Carpenter received the V.C. 'for most conspicuous gallantry' on April 23, 1918).

Once it had been decided to make an attack on the Mole, we had to have a large number of men to carry it out, and to obtain suitable ships. So the Grand Fleet, the main naval depots, and the various Commands, were asked to lend a certain number of the most suitable men they had. These men were given to understand that they were going on a hazardous enterprise, so far as I know, and therefore one can say that they volunteered for it, although they were not actually told at the time what they were going to do.

★★★★★★

The Zeebrugge Mole, along with the harbour and canal, was built, at a cost of nearly 42,000,000 *francs*, between 1895 and 1907. The Mole is constructed mainly of concrete blocks. The canal is 280 feet wide and 25 feet deep.

For the contribution of the various Commands see the Dispatch of May 9, para. 31.

Lieutenant-Commander Hilton Young gives the wording of the invitation: 'Volunteers are wanted for an undertaking of real danger' (*Cornhill Magazine*, December 1918).

They were all picked men—picked from volunteers. We tried them out under intensive training until we got exactly the men we wanted. That, naturally, was a long and anxious job. At first they thought it was for a hazardous operation in France, and they were keen enough then; but later, when we entrusted them with the real secret, and they knew we were after Zeebrugge and Ostend, there was no holding them!'—Statement by Captain Carpenter in Keble Howard's *The Glory of Zeebrugge* (1918).

An Admiralty official, quoted in the *Daily Mail* of April 26, states: 'When the preparations were completed the volunteers were sent on board their ships, and for three weeks, while waiting for the favourable moment, never a man was allowed ashore.'

The Dispatch of May 9, para. 30, speaks of 'anxious days of waiting in crowded ships in a secluded (West Swin) anchorage' from April 4 onwards, (para. 33).

★★★★★★

However, before the operation actually took place, every man had to be informed quite clearly what was expected of him, because one fully realised that every officer might be knocked out and the men would be entirely on their own. Then the men undoubtedly had a chance of saying that they did not want to go, perhaps for family reasons; but, so far as I know, there was not a single case of a man asking to be left behind. To my knowledge, in fact, in one ship (the *Intrepid*), where orders had been given that certain men were to be left behind, those men in almost a mutinous spirit came up before their captain and said they absolutely refused to leave the ship. As it happened, in this particular case, owing to a slight hitch, the extra crew of this ship were not taken off. (The statement applies also to *Iphigenia*. See Dispatch of May 9, para. 95, 96). The whole of the men went into Zeebrugge Canal in the block-ship, and the whole of them were saved and brought back.

The nature of the operation was such that it required the use of a very large number of small craft; and the trip across the sea being rather over a hundred miles each way made it necessary that the weather should be fine. (*I. e.* from the Swin to Zeebrugge. The Swin was left at 1.10 p.m., the point of concentration-63 miles-at 4.53 p.m. Steaming at ten knots the full distance took nearly eleven hours to accomplish).

At the same time the wind had to be on-shore, so that we could use our smoke-screens effectively. At the same time, too, the operation had to be carried out at high water, so as to allow the block-ships to get in. Again, owing to the presence of a large number of German guns on the Belgian coast it was necessary to carry out the operation at night; and it was fully realised that if it were carried out in the latter part of the night—that is to say, by the morning twilight—there was practically no chance of any ship getting away in the early morning, when they could be seen from the shore.

★★★★★★

The Germans had at least 120 guns of heavy calibre in position on the 12 miles of coast separating Ostend from Zeebrugge.
It was estimated that it would take *Vindictive* and her escort one hour and twenty minutes to get out of range on their return journey, and that half an hour before sunrise the vis-

ibility would be good enough to enable the German batteries to spot them. Hence, it was calculated that the ships must leave the Mole at latest one hour and fifty minutes before sunrise.— *Nineteenth Century*, June 1918. Approximately, sunrise at Ostend and Zeebrugge on April 23, 1918, was at 4.40 a.m. G.M.T. The latest moment for departure, therefore, was 2 50 a.m. The programme fixed it for 1.40 a.m. In fact, *Vindictive* left at 1.10 a.m.)

★★★★★★

It was, therefore, a rather complicated combination of conditions that we required, and during the period that we were waiting for a suitable day, (from April 4), the disappointments were very great. Before the operation took place we had all gone over to within a few miles of our objectives and had to turn back owing to impossible weather conditions suddenly arising, (on April 11-12), and it was with very anxious hearts that we waited for suitable weather conditions to occur, realising that every day we waited made a greater chance for the news of the impending operation to leak out and get across to Germany, and for preparations to be made over there to defeat the operation at the outset. The chances of the vicinities of Zeebrugge and Ostend being heavily mined were considerable, and the risk of this had to be taken. (Special arrangements were made for the salvage of crews and landing parties in the event of vessels being mined. See Dispatch of May 9, para. 17).

At last (April 22) the opportunity we had waited for so long arose, and everybody started off in the highest spirits and with no other thought than to make the very greatest success of the operation that we could possibly do. Fate was very kind to us on the whole, and everything went well, almost as per schedule.

★★★★★★

The weather conditions broke down at the last moment and contributed to defeat the Ostend attack. On the other hand, the expedition encountered neither an unexpected mine field, nor scouting vessels, nor scouting planes to give warning. Nor did better conditions recur.

★★★★★★

The various phases of the operation depended on accurate timing of the work of the various units.

★★★★★★

One of the most noteworthy features of the operation, as Staff-Paymaster Cox points out (*Nineteenth Century*, June 1918), was the marvellous punctuality shown by the co-operating units: bombardment by monitors and coast-batteries at 11.20 p.m.; the fog-raising motor-boats to begin operations at 11.40 p.m.; *Vindictive* and her escort to close the Mole at 12 a.m.; the submarine attack to cut the Mole from shore reinforcements at 12.15 a.m.; the leading block-ship to pass the lighthouse at 12.25 a.m.; and lastly the motor-craft to pick up the crews of the scuttled ships.

******

The smoke-screen craft and the fast motor-boats at given intervals rushed on ahead at full speed, laid their smoke-screens, attacked enemy vessels (in the harbour) with torpedoes, and generally cleared the way for the main force, in addition to hiding the approach of the latter from the shore batteries. Meanwhile a heavy bombardment was being carried out by our monitors, and the sound of their firing as we approached was one of the most heartening things that I can remember. On arriving at a certain point some considerable distance from shore the forces parted, some going to Zeebrugge and some to Ostend, the idea being that the forces should arrive at the two places simultaneously, so that communication from one place to the other could not be used as a warning in either case. (According to the Press Bureau Narrative the distance was about 15 miles).

At precisely at midnight the main force arrived at Zeebrugge and two of the block-ships, (H.M.S. *Sirius* and *Brilliant*), arrived at Ostend.

At midnight we (*Vindictive*) steamed through a very thick smoke-screen. German star-shells were lighting up the whole place almost like daylight, and one had an extraordinary naked feeling when one saw how exposed we were, although it was in the middle of the night. On emerging from the smoke-screen the end of the Mole, where the lighthouse is, was seen close ahead, distant about 400 yards. The ship was turned immediately to go alongside and increased to full speed so as to get there as fast as possible. We had decided not to open fire from the ship until they opened fire on us, so that we might remain unobserved to the last possible moment. A battery of five or six guns on the Mole began firing at us almost immediately from a range of about 300 yards, and every gun on the *Vindictive* that would bear fired at them as hard as it could.

******1

H.M.S. *Vindictive*, light cruiser, launched 1897, completed 1898; 20 knots; normal complement 430; ten 6-inch and also smaller

35

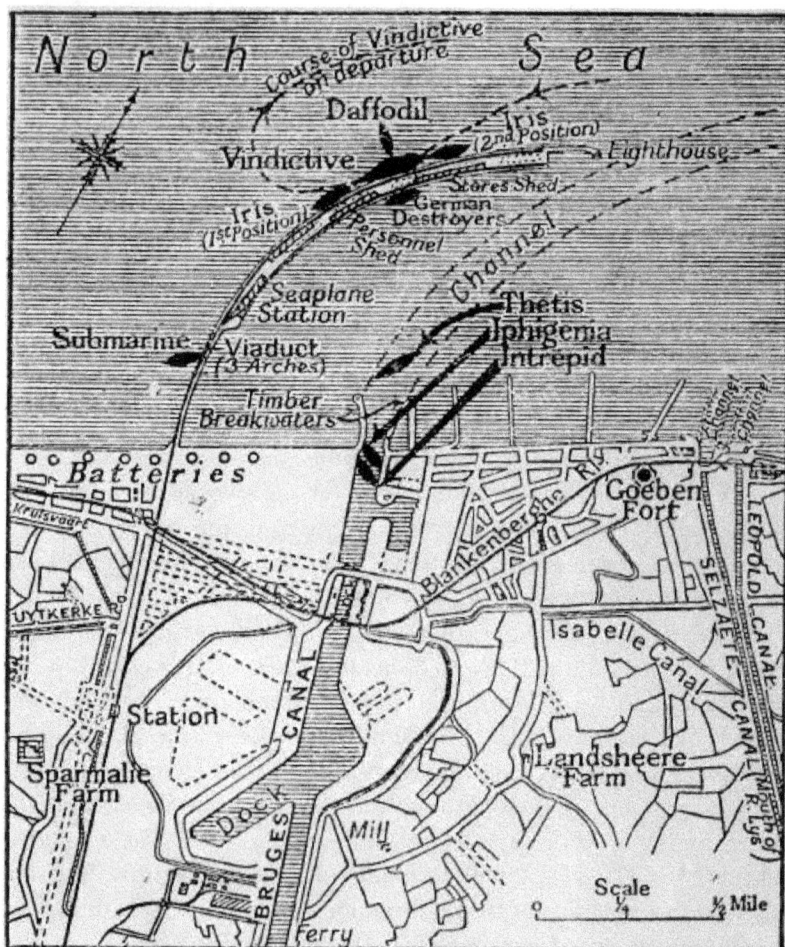

PLAN OF THE ZEEBRUGGE RAID, APRIL 23.
Note.—The precise positions of the British ships are shown
in the official plan

guns; with the Mediterranean Fleet 1900-4; thereafter in Dock-yard Reserve; commissioned for service in the Nore Division of Home Fleet; served successively in 3rd and 4th Divisions of Home Fleet and as tender to H.M.S. *Albion* and H.M.S. *Vernon*. At 11.56 p.m. *Vindictive* saw the Mole about 300 yards distant on the port bow. (Dispatch, para. 60).

The *London Gazette of* July 23, 1918, announcing Captain Carpenter's distinction, states: 'When *Vindictive* was within a few yards of the Mole the enemy started and maintained a heavy fire from batteries, machine-guns, and rifles on to the bridge.'

In the *Cornhill* article already quoted Lieut.-Commander Hilton Young writes: 'We were some 600 yards from the Mole, and had just begun to turn to starboard to run alongside it, when the storm broke. A searchlight shone out from the end of the Mole, swung to left and right, and settled on the ship. At once the guns of the Mole battery opened fire.' The battery had been reckoned to be of 4.1-in. guns. They proved to be 5.9's. Three of the six guns on the extension were 4.1's. See the Dispatch, para. 56, 71.

★★★★★★

In less than five minutes the ship was alongside the Mole, and efforts were made to grapple the Mole so as to keep the ship in place. The *Daffodil*, which was following close astern, came up, and in the most gallant manner placed her bow against the *Vindictive* and pushed the *Vindictive* sideways until she was close alongside the Mole. There was a very heavy swell against the Mole. The ships were rolling about, and this made the work of securing to the Mole exceedingly difficult.

★★★★★★

Timed to arrive at 12 o'clock a.m. G.M.T., *Vindictive* actually made alongside the Mole at 12.1 a.m. Captain Carpenter was directed to fetch up 400 yards nearer the head of the Mole than the position he actually took. Consequently, the 6.9 battery at the end of the Mole was not put out of action completely. The plan contemplated the landing parties storming the Mole on the top of the battery. See Dispatch, para. 71.

It is wrongly stated in *How we Twisted the Dragon's Tail*, that the special Mole anchors 'proved too short for the job'. See the Dispatch, para. 62.

Daffodil arrived at 12.4 a.m. See the Dispatch, para. 62.

Captain Carpenter does not mention *Iris*. She first attempted to

37

make fast to the Mole ahead of *Vindictive*. The heavy swell prevented her, and after heroic efforts she fell astern of *Vindictive* and began to land her parties over the cruiser. See the Dispatch, para. 63.

★★★★★★

When the brows were run out from the *Vindictive* the men at once climbed out along them.

★★★★★★

To facilitate landing on the outer wall of the Mole, where landings are not wont to be made. *Vindictive* carried a false top-deck along her port side, that is, on the left side looking forward. From this false deck eighteen brows, or landing gangways, wore operated, over which the storming parties could pass on to the Mole. Captain Carpenter describes a brow as 'a sort of light drawbridge with a hinge in the middle.' (*The Glory of Zeebrugge)*. Its construction and appearance are easily realised from the illustration.

★★★★★★

It was an extremely perilous task, in view of the fact that the ends of the brows at one moment were from 8 ft. to 10 ft. above the wall and the next moment were crashing on the wall as the ship rolled. (In fact their weight kept them always resting on the parapet. They sawed backwards and forwards with the ship's motion). The way in which the men got over those brows was almost superhuman. I expected every moment to see them falling off between the Mole and the ship—at least a 30-ft. drop—and being crushed by the ship against the wall. But not a man fell; their agility was wonderful. It was not a case of seamen running barefoot along the deck of a rolling ship; the men were carrying heavy accoutrements, bombs, Lewis guns, and other articles, and their path lay along a narrow and extremely unsteady plank. They never hesitated. They went along the brows and on to the Mole with the utmost possible speed. Within a few minutes three to four hundred had been landed, (German Admiralty's account mendaciously states the number as forty, all of whom are said to have been taken alive or dead!), and under cover of a barrage put down on the Mole by Stokes guns and howitzer fire from the ship they fought their way along.

★★★★★★

An addendum to Captain Carpenter's narrative states that *Vindictive's* howitzers were trained on the Goeben Fort (east of the

Canal mouth), the dock-gates inside the Canal mouth, and the shore batteries near the landward end of the Mole. The forward howitzer was put out of action and its crew suffered severely.

★★★★★★

Comparatively few of the German guns were able to hit the hull of the ship, as it was behind the protection of the wall. Safety, in fact, depended on how near you could get to the enemy guns instead of how far away. While the hull was guarded, the upper works of the ship—the funnels, masts, ventilators, and bridge—were showing above the wall, and on these a large number of German guns appeared to be concentrated. Many of our casualties were caused by splinters coming down from the upper works. If it had not been for the *Daffodil* continuing to push the ship in towards the wall throughout the operation none of the men who went on the Mole would ever have got back again.

★★★★★★

'Those chaps in the fighting-top were attracting a lot of attention, and the Huns were constantly trying to drop a shell amongst them. They succeeded at last, I'm sorry to say, and laid out every man-jack but one—Sergeant Finch. He was wounded badly, but dragged himself out from under the bodies of his pals and went on working his little gun until he couldn't work it any longer.'—Captain Carpenter's statement in *The Glory of Zeebrugge*. Finch kept up his fire until the fighting-top was destroyed by a direct hit. He received the V.C.

Daffodil managed to develop double her normal steam-pressure for the purpose. Eventually she landed her storming party over *Vindictive*.

★★★★★★

About twenty-five minutes after the *Vindictive* got alongside, the block-ships were seen rounding the lighthouse and heading for the canal entrance. It was then realised on board the *Iris, Daffodil*, and *Vindictive* that their work had been accomplished. A quarter of an hour after the *Vindictive* took her position, and just before the blockers arrived, a tremendous explosion was seen at the shore end of the Mole. We then knew that our submarine had managed to get herself in between the piles of the viaduct connecting the Mole with the shore and had blown herself up.

★★★★★★

Vindictive got alongside the Mole at 12.1 a.m. G.M.T. The leading block-ship passed the actual Mole end at 12.25.

At 12.20 a.m. G.M.T. See accounts of Submarine C 3's performance, and the Dispatch, para. 23, 8Cff.

'I never saw such a column of flame! It seemed a mile high.' (Captain Carpenter, in *The Glory of Zeebrugge*.)

★★★★★★

She carried several tons of high explosive, and the effect of her action was effectually to cut off the Mole from the land. Before the explosion the crew of the submarine, which comprised some half-dozen officers and men, (Lieutenant R. D. Sandford, R.N., in command, Lieutenant J. Howell-Price, D.S.C., R.N.R., Stoker H. C. Bindall, P.O. Walter Harner, Leading Seaman W. G. Cleaver, Engine-room Artificer A. G. Roxburgh), got away in a very small motor skiff, which lost its propeller and had to be pulled with paddles against a heavy tide and under machine-gun fire from a range which could be reckoned only in feet. Most of the crew were wounded, but the tiny boat was picked up by a steam-pinnace, (commanded by Lieutenant Sandford's brother, Lieut. -Commander F. H. Sandford. See Dispatch, para. 91).

It is possible that the Germans, who saw the submarine coming in under the play of their searchlights, thought that her object was to attack the vessels within the Mole and that she thought it feasible to get through the viaduct (into the harbour basin) to do this. Their neglect to stop the submarine as she approached could only be put down to the fact that they knew she could not get through, owing to the large amount of interlacing between the piles, and that they really believed they were catching her.

★★★★★★

The open passage from outside to within the harbour had been covered over with a sort of steel curtain, leaving a hole for the tide to run through. The submarine made for the hole.—Statement by Lieutenant-Commander Sandford in *The Glory of Zeebrugge*. The explosion, according to the Press Bureau account, made a gap of more than 100 ft. in the structure. See Dispatch, para. 88).

★★★★★★

A large number of Germans were actually on the viaduct a few feet above the submarine, and were firing at her with machine-guns. I think it can safely be said that every one of those Germans went up with the viaduct. The cheer raised by my men in the *Vindictive* when they saw the terrific explosion was one of the finest things I ever

40

heard. Many of the men were severely wounded—some had three and even four wounds—but they had no thought except for the success of the operation.

The block-ships came under very heavy fire immediately they rounded the end of the Mole. Most of the fire, it appears, was concentrated on the leading ship, the *Thetis*. She ran ashore off the entrance to the canal on the (western) edge of the channel, and was sunk as approximately as possible across the channel itself, thus forming an obstruction to the passage of the German vessels. Before going down she gave a signal to the other two block-ships, which were following close behind, to inform them which side of her to pass in order to get to the canal entrance. This co-operation between the three block-ships, carried out under extremely heavy fire, was one of the finest things of the operation. The second and third ships, the *Intrepid* and *Iphigenia*, both went straight through the canal entrance until they actually reached a point some two or three hundred yards inside the shore lines, and behind some of the German batteries.

★★★★★★

H.M.S. *Thetis, Intrepid*, and *Iphigenia* were sister ships of the *Apollo* class, launched about 1891, displacing about 3,600 tons each, and latterly used as mine-layers.
The explanation of her mishap is given by the Press Bureau account, and the Dispatch, para. 94.
See the sea-plane photograph. *Iphigenia*, last of the block-ships, was sunk at 12.45 a.m. See Dispatch, para. 24.

★★★★★★

It really seems very wonderful. How the crews of the two ships ever got away is almost beyond imagination. A motor-launch seems to have picked up the majority of them in an extraordinarily gallant way under extremely heavy fire from very short range. (Lieutenant P. T. Dean, R.N.V.R. One M.L. followed each block-ship. No. 110 was sunk rounding the Mole. No. 526 brought away the crew of *Thetis*. Lieutenant Dean, following *Iphigenia* in No. 282, rescued 101 men from *Iphigenia* and *Intrepid*). The launch got clear and put the crews on board destroyers. A number of other men escaped by their own boats. They had to pull several miles out to sea, and were then picked up by vessels outside.

The situation rather more than an hour after the *Vindictive* got alongside was this: The block-ships had passed in, had come to the end of their run, and had done their work. The viaduct was blown up

Sea Plane view of the Zeebrugge lock gates
showing position of sunken cruisers

and the Mole had been stormed. (Dispatch, para. 67 ff.) Nothing but a useless sacrifice of life could have followed if the three boarding vessels had remained by the Mole any longer. The signal to withdraw was therefore given, and the ships got away under cover of their smoke-screens as quickly as they could. I have already told you that owing to the ships being so close to the German guns, that is to say, right alongside the wall, they were comparatively immune from hits.

But it was realised that as soon as we left the shelter of the wall we should come under exceedingly heavy fire. I doubt whether there was anybody on board who really thought we should get back. The signal for the re-embarkation of the landing parties was given by siren, but the noise of the guns was so loud that it had to be repeated many times. (*Daffodil's* siren made the signal at 12.50 a.m. *Vindictive's* searchlights, which had been intended to give twenty minutes' warning, had been destroyed, as well as her siren which was to have given the executive signal, see the Dispatch, para. 104).

Twenty minutes passed before it was definitely reported that there was nobody left on the Mole who could possibly get on the withdrawing ships. All three ships got away from the wall. They went at full speed and were followed all the way along their course by salvos from the German guns. Shells seemed to fall all round the ships without actually hitting them. The gunners apparently had our speed but not our range, and with remarkable regularity the salvos plopped into the sea behind us. In a short time, the ships were clear of imminent danger owing to the large amount of smoke which they had left behind them.

★★★★★★

Approximately 1.10 a.m. G.M.T. *Vindictive* was clear at 1.15 a.m. One hour and nine minutes was the precise duration of *Vindictive's* stay alongside the Mole. There is a careful account of the operation in *A Light Ship* (1918) by 'Taffrail'.

The statement is true of *Vindictive* (see Lieut.-Commander Hilton Young's article in the *Cornhill Magazine* for Dec. 1918), but not of *Iris*. Sir Roger Keyes's Dispatch of May 9 (para. 105) says: 'Shortly after leaving the Mole the ship came under a very heavy fire from the Mole and shore batteries, being hit tea times by small shell and twice by large ones. The first large shell carried away the port side of the bridge.'

'At that short range—400 or 500 yards', writes Lieut.-Commander Hilton Young, 'the light fabric of the little ship was hulled through and through, flames and smoke spurting from

43

her far side as the shells struck. I thought at the time that she had probably sunk.'

Captain Carpenter omits to mention the gallant conduct of the small craft, which got between the three ships and the shore batteries and made clouds of smoke.

★★★★★★

Should the Germans, who appear to suffer from an extreme gift of imagination, ever suggest that the *Vindictive* did not get alongside the Mole, their story could easily be refuted by the fact that we brought away a piece of Zeebrugge Mole, weighing about a quarter of a ton, which fell on my ship. (According to a statement in the *Morning Post* of April 20, 1918, it is intended to use part of this relic for a memorial of the dead who fell in the Raid).

On the way across, before the operation, the admiral made the signal to the *Vindictive*, "St. George for England!" and the reply was made to him, "May we give the Dragon's tail a damned good twist". I think we succeeded in doing it.'

(b) THE PRESS BUREAU NARRATIVE.

(The complete text is in the *Morning Post*, April 26, 1918, and *The Glory of Zeebrugge*)'.

April 24, 1918.

Those who recall High Wood upon the Somme—and they must be many—as it was after the battles of 1916, may easily figure to themselves the decks of His Majesty's Ship *Vindictive* as she lies to-day, (1919), a stark, black profile against the sea haze of the harbour at Dover amid the stripped, trim shapes of the fighting ships which throng these waters. That wilderness of debris, that litter of the used and broken tools of war, that lavish ruin, and that prodigal evidence of death and battle, are as obvious and plentiful here as there. The ruined tank nosing at the stout tree which stopped it has its parallel in the flamethrower hut at the port wing of *Vindictive's* bridge, its iron sides freckled with rents from machine-gun bullets and shell-splinters. The tall white cross which commemorates the martyrdom of the London-ers is sister to the dingy pierced White Ensign which floated over the fight on the Zeebrugge Mole.

Looking aft from the chaos of her wrecked bridge, one sees, snug against their wharf, the heroic bourgeois shapes of the two Liverpool ferry-boats (their captains' quarters are still labelled "Ladies Only") *Iris* and *Daffodil*, which shared with *Vindictive* the honours and ardours of

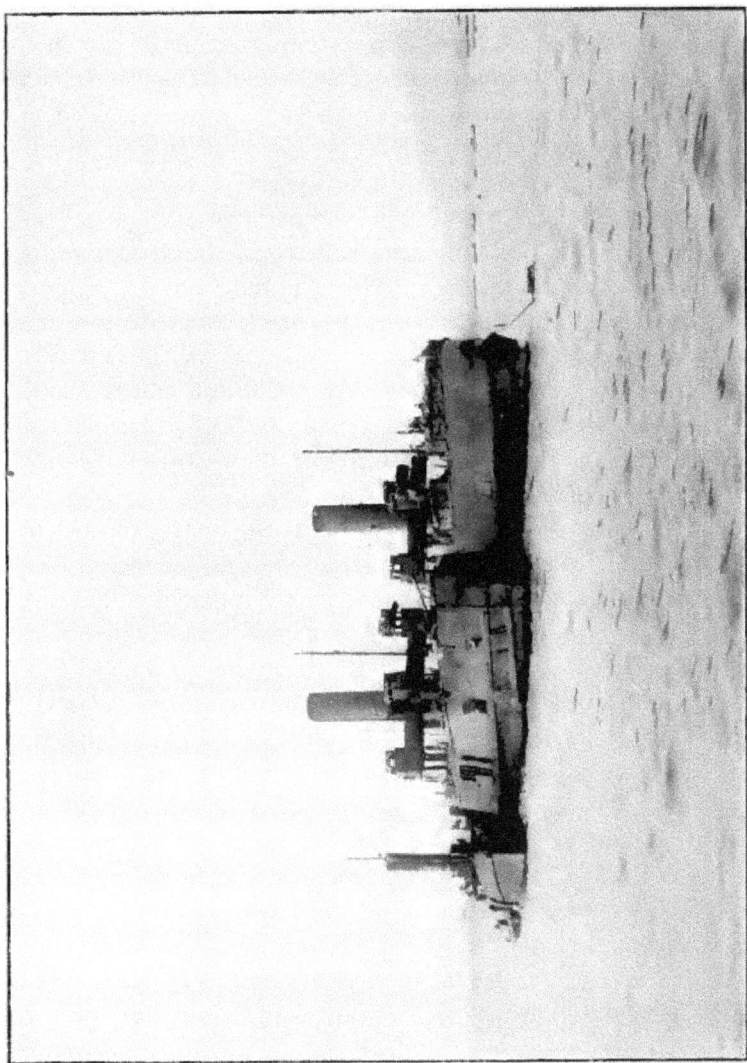

The Mersey ferryboats, *Iris* (right) and *Daffodil* (centre)

the fight. The epic of their achievement shapes itself in the light of that view across the scarred and littered decks, in that environment of grey water and great still ships.

Their objectives were the canal of Zeebrugge and the entrance to the harbour of Ostend—theirs, and those of five other veteran and obsolete cruisers and a mosquito fleet of destroyers, motor-launches, and coastal motorboats. Three of the cruisers. *Intrepid, Iphigenia,* and *Thetis,* each duly packed with concrete and with mines attached to her bottom for the purpose of sinking her, *Merrimac*-fashion, in the neck of the canal, were aimed at Zeebrugge; two others, similarly prepared, were directed at Ostend. (The *Merrimac,* commanded by Naval Constructor Hobson, was sunk in Santiago Harbour, during the Spanish-American War, on June 3, 1898). The function of *Vindictive,* with her ferryboats, was to attack the great half-moon Mole which guards the Zeebrugge Canal, land blue-jackets and marines upon it, destroy what stores, guns, and Germans she could find, and generally create a diversion while the block-ships ran in and sank themselves in their appointed place. Vice-Admiral Keyes, in the destroyer *Warwick,* commanded the operation.

There had been two previous attempts at the attack, capable of being pushed home if weather and other conditions had served. The night of the 22nd of April offered nearly all the required conditions, and at some fifteen miles off Zeebrugge the ships took up their formation for the attack. *Vindictive,* which had been towing *Iris* and *Daffodil,* cast them off to follow under their own steam; *Intrepid, Iphigenia,* and *Thetis* slowed down to give the first three time to get alongside the Mole; *Sirius* and *Brilliant* shifted their course for Ostend; and the great swarm of destroyers and motor-craft sowed themselves abroad upon their multifarious particular duties. The night was overcast, and there was a drift of haze; down the coast a great searchlight swung its beam to and fro; there was a small wind and a short sea.

From *Vindictive's* bridge, as she headed in towards the Mole, with her faithful ferry-boats at her heels, there was scarcely a glimmer of light to be seen shorewards. Ahead of her, as she drove through the water, rolled the smoke-screen, her cloak of invisibility, wrapped about her by the small craft. This was a device of Wing-Commander Brock, R.N.A.S., "without which", acknowledges the Admiral in Command, "the operation could not have been conducted." The north-east wind moved the volume of it shoreward ahead of the ships; beyond it, the distant town and its defenders were unsuspicious; and it was not till

Vindictive, with her blue-jackets and marines standing ready for the landing, was close upon the Mole that the wind lulled and came away again from the south-west, sweeping back the smoke-screen and laying her bare to the eyes that looked seaward.

★★★★★★

Wing-Commander Frank Arthur Brock, R.A.F., b. 1884; director of Messrs. C. T. Brock & Co., firework manufacturers; Flight-Commander, R.A.F., 1916; O.B.E., January 1918; a man of marked inventive genius. He invented the first powerful flares used for the Channel barrage (see a statement by Sir Roger Keyes in *The Times* of December 13, 1918). See the Dispatch, para. 37, on the 'fog' preparations.

Lieut.-Commander Hilton Young (*Cornhill Magazine*, December 1918) describes the scene: 'The sky was thick with a perfect rain of star-shells; but, clearly as they showed us to ourselves, it did not follow that they showed us to the Germans. As each star fell into the smoke-screen that now covered the sea, unless it was within a very few hundred yards of us it was eclipsed as a star and became a large vague nebula. Although there was plenty of light about, a few hundred yards from the ship (*Vindictive*) everything was blotted out in wreaths, eddies and whirls of glowing vapour.'

★★★★★★

There was a moment immediately afterwards when it seemed to those in the ships as if the dim coast and the hidden harbour exploded into light. A star-shell soared aloft, then a score of star-shells; the wavering beams of the searchlights swung round and settled to a glare; the wildfire of gun-flashes leapt against the sky; strings of luminous green beads shot aloft, hung, and sank; and the darkness of the night was supplanted by the nightmare daylight of battle-fires. Guns and machine-guns along the Mole and batteries ashore woke to life, and it was in a gale of shelling that *Vindictive* laid her nose against the thirty-foot high concrete side of the Mole, let go an anchor and signed to *Daffodil* to shove her stern in. *Iris* went ahead and endeavoured to get alongside likewise.

★★★★★★

It seems that *Vindictive* was about twenty minutes from the Mole when the Germans sent up the warning star-shell. This estimate is confirmed by Lieut.-Commander Hilton Young in the *Cornhill Magazine*, December 1918.

'Green beads' generally called 'flaming onions'.
See the Dispatch, para. 62, for *Vindictive's* difficulties here.

★★★★★★

The fire, from the account of everybody concerned, was intense. While the ships plunged and rolled beside the Mole in an unexpected scend of sea, *Vindictive* with her greater draught jarring against the foundation of the Mole with every plunge, they were swept diagonally by machine-gun fire from both ends of the Mole and by heavy batteries ashore. Commander A. F. B. Carpenter (now captain) conned *Vindictive* from her open bridge till her stern was laid in, when he took up his position in the flame-thrower hut on the port side. It is to this hut that reference has already been made; it is marvellous that any occupant of it should have survived a minute, so riddled and shattered is it." (See picture further on). Officers of *Iris*, which was in trouble ahead of *Vindictive*, describe Captain Carpenter as "handling her like a picket-boat".

Vindictive was fitted along the port side with a high false deck, whence ran the eighteen brows, or gangways, by which the storming and demolition parties were to land.

★★★★★★

An officer of the landing party (quoted in *The Times*, April 25, 1918) states that only two proved serviceable for landing purposes, the remainder having been shot away. Two others were got into order. Secethe Dispatch, para. 62.

The primary object of the attack on the Mole was the capture of the 5.9-in. battery at its sea end, a serious menace to the passage of the block-ships. A secondary object was to damage the material on the Mole in the time required for blocking the canal, and to distract the enemy's attention in some degree from the main operation, *i.e.* the sinking of the block-ships. The Mole attack consisted of (a) the landing of storming and demolition parties at the sea end, and (b) the destruction of the iron viaduct connecting the Mole with the shore.

★★★★★★

The men were gathered in readiness on the main and lower decks, while Colonel Elliot, (Lieutenant-Colonel Bertram Nowel Elliot, D.S.O.), who was to lead the marines, waited on the false deck just abaft the bridge, and Captain H. C. Halahan, (Captain Henry Crosby Halahan, D.S.O., R.N.), who commanded the bluejackets, was amidships. The gangways were lowered, and scraped and rebounded upon the high parapet of the Mole as *Vindictive* rolled; and the word for the assault had not yet been given when both leaders were killed, Colonel Elliot by a shell, and Captain Halahan by the machine-gun fire which swept the decks. The same shell that killed Colonel Elliot also did fearful execution in the forward Stokes Mortar Battery.

"The men were magnificent." Every officer bears the same testimony. The mere landing on the Mole was a perilous business; it involved a passage across the crashing, splintering gangways, a drop over the parapet into the field of fire of the German machine-guns, which swept its length, (this drop about four feet on to a ledge, about eight feet wide, with an iron railing on the harbour-side, which runs along the inner wall of the Mole), and a further drop of some 15 ft. to the surface of the Mole itself. (See Dispatch, para. 72).

Many were killed and more were wounded as they crowded up to the gangways; but nothing hindered the orderly and speedy landing by every gangway. Lieutenant H. T. C. Walker had his arm carried away by a shell on the upper deck, and lay in the darkness while the storming parties trod him under. He was recognised and dragged aside by the commander (Carpenter). He raised his remaining arm in greeting. "Good luck to you," he called, as the rest of the stormers hastened by; "good luck!"

The lower deck was a shambles as the commander made the rounds of his ship; yet those wounded and dying raised themselves to cheer as he made his tour. The crew of the howitzer which was mounted forward had all been killed; a second crew was destroyed likewise; and even then a third crew was taking over the gun. (Dispatch, para. 64). In the stern cabin a firework expert who had never been to sea before—one of Captain Brock's employees—was steadily firing great illuminating rockets out of a scuttle to show up the lighthouse on the end of the Mole to the block-ships and their escort. (*Thetis* was much aided by this. See Dispatch, para. 91).

Daffodil, after aiding to berth *Vindictive*, should have proceeded to land her own men, but now Commander Carpenter ordered her to remain as she was, with her bows against *Vindictive's* quarter, pressing the latter ship into the Mole. (*Daffodil* should have come alongside *Vindictive* to land her parties. But having to shore *Vindictive* on to the Mole during the whole operation, *Daffodil's* men had to disembark from her bows on to *Vindictive*. See Dispatch, para. 62).

Normally *Daffodil's* boilers develop eighty pounds' pressure of steam per inch; but now, for this particular task, Artificer-Engineer

Sutton, in charge of them, maintained a hundred and sixty pounds for the whole period that she was holding *Vindictive* to the Mole. Her casualties, owing to her position during the fight, were small—one man killed and eight wounded, among them her commander, Lieutenant H. Campbell, who was struck in the right eye by a shell splinter.

★★★★★★

Art.-Engineer William Mark Sutton, R.N., received the D.S.C. For this and other decorated officers' record of service see the *London Gazette* of July 23, 1918.

Had not *Daffodil* been so employed *Vindictive* could not have been held in position at the Mole nor the landing parties have been able to return to the ship.

Lieutenant Harold George Campbell, R.N., received the D.S.O.

★★★★★★

Iris had troubles of her own. Her first attempts to make fast to the Mole ahead of *Vindictive* failed, as her grapnels were not large enough to span the parapet, (this is not accurate). Two officers, Lieutenant-Commander Bradford and Lieutenant Hawkings, climbed ashore and sat astride the parapet trying to make the grapnels fast till each was killed and fell down between the ship and the wall. Commander Valentine Gibbs had both legs shot away, and died next morning. Lieutenant Spencer, R.N.R., though wounded, took command, and refused to be relieved. *Iris* was obliged at last to change her position, and fall in astern of *Vindictive*, and suffered very heavily from the fire.

★★★★★★★

Lt.-Commander G. N. Bradford, R.N. He was the first to set foot on the Mole, writes Lieutenant-Commander Hilton Young (*Cornhill Magazine*, Dec. 1918). He climbed up a davit and jumped ashore. See the Dispatch, para. 72.

Lieutenant C. E.V. Hawkings, K.N.

Commander Valentine Francis Gibbs, R.N.

Lieutenant G. Spencer, D.S.C, R.N.R.; died of wounds. The statement in the text needs correction. Lieutenant Spencer, who was acting as navigator, lay severely wounded on the remnants of the bridge, conning the ship away from the Mole. Lieutenant Oscar Henderson, representing the Portsmouth Command, promptly went up and took command. He received the D.S.O. See the Dispatch, para. 105.

Lieutenant-Commander Hilton Young writes (*Cornhill Magazine*, Dec. 1918): 'Now, the *Iris* was going to try to land her parties over the *Vindictive*. But beside the *Vindictive* the *Iris* danced in the swell like a cork, and it was some time before we could get a hawser on board from her, or secure it when we had got it. At last it was done, and the men in the *Iris*, watching their opportunity, began to jump into the *Vindictive*. But meanwhile time had fled. We seemed to have been alongside a few minutes only; we had been there an hour, and it was almost time to go.' See the Dispatch, para. 63.

★★★★★★

A single big shell plunged through the upper deck and burst below at a point where fifty-six marines were awaiting the order to go to the gangways. Forty-nine were killed, and the remaining seven wounded. Another shell in the ward-room, which was serving as sick-bay, killed four officers and twenty-six men. Her total casualties were eight officers and sixty-nine men killed and three officers and a hundred and two men wounded.

The storming and demolition-parties upon the Mole met with no resistance from the Germans, other than the intense and unremitting fire. The geography of the great Mole, with its railway line and its many buildings, hangars, and store-sheds, was already well known, and the demolition-parties moved to their appointed work in perfect order. One after another the buildings burst into flame or split and crumbled as the dynamite went off. (The statement is incorrect). A bombing party, working up towards the Mole extension in search of the enemy, destroyed several machine-gun emplacements, but not a single prisoner rewarded them.

It appears that on the approach of the ships and with the opening of the fire, the enemy simply retired and contented themselves with bringing machine-guns to the shore end of the Mole. And while they worked and destroyed, the covering party below the parapet could see in the harbour, by the light of the German star-shells, the shapes of the block-ships stealing in and out of their own smoke and making for the mouth of the canal.

Thetis came first, steaming into a tornado of shell from the great batteries ashore. All her crew, save a remnant who remained to steam her in and sink her, had already been taken off her by the ubiquitous motor-launches, but the remnant spared hands enough to keep her four guns going. It was hers to show the road to *Intrepid* and *Iphigenia*, who followed. She cleared the string of armed barges which defends the channel from the tip of the Mole, but had the ill-fortune to foul one of her propellers upon the net-defence which flanks it on the shore side. The propeller gathered in the net and rendered her practically unmanageable; the shore batteries found her and pounded her unremittingly; she bumped into a bank, edged off, and found herself in the channel again, still some hundreds of yards from the mouth of the canal, in a practically sinking condition. As she lay she signalled invaluable directions to the others, and here Commander R. S. Sneyd, D.S.O., accordingly blew the charges and sank her.

★★★★★★

Before going down *Thetis* signalled to her consorts to pass to starboard of her by firing a green rocket. Engineer Lieutenant-Commander Ronald Charles Boddie restarted her starboard engine, thereby enabling the ship to be turned into the fairway before she sank. He received the D.S.O. See *The Navy Eternal*, and Sir Roger Keyes's Dispatch, para. 94.

Commander Ralph S. Sneyd, D.S.O., R.N., specially promoted to Captain for services in action.

★★★★★★

A motor-launch, (No. 526), under Lieutenant H. Littleton, R.N.V.R., raced alongside and took off her crew. Her losses were five killed and five wounded. (Lieutenant Hugh Alexander Littleton, R.N.V.R., received the D.S.O.).

Intrepid, smoking like a volcano and with all her guns blazing, followed; her motor-launch had failed to get alongside outside the harbour, and she had men enough for anything. Straight into the canal she steered, her smoke blowing back from her into *Iphigenia's* eyes, so that the latter, blinded and going a little wild, rammed a dredger with a barge moored beside it, which lay at the western arm of the canal. She got clear, though, and entered the canal, pushing the barge before her. It was then that a shell hit the steam connexions of her whistle, and the escape of steam which followed drove off some of the smoke and let her see what she was doing.

Lieutenant Stuart Bonham-Carter, commanding the *Intrepid*, placed the nose of his ship neatly on the mud of the western bank, (*i.e.* on his starboard-right-side looking forward), ordered his crew away, and blew up his ship by the switches in the chart-room. (Lieutenant Stuart Sumner Bonham-Carter, R.N., received the D.S.O.). Four dull bumps were all that could be heard, and immediately afterwards there arrived on deck the engineer, who had been in the engine-room during the explosion, and reported that all was as it should be. (As the ship was making stern way Lieut. Bonham-Carter had to blow the charges before the steaming party could get out of the engine-room. See the Dispatch, para. 95).

Lieutenant E. W. Billyard-Leake, commanding *Iphigenia*, beached her according to arrangement on the eastern side, blew her up, saw her drop nicely across the canal, and left her with her engines still going to hold her in position till she should have bedded well down on the bottom.

★★★★★★

Lieutenant Edward Whaley Billyard-Leake, R.N., received the D.S.O. Lieut. Ivan B. Franks, R.N., who had superintended the early preparations of all the block-ships, and had commanded *Iphigenia* on the occasion of the two abandoned attempts, was laid low by appendicitis two days before the actual attack. See the Dispatch, para. 40.

At 12.45 a.m. Sir Roger Keyes in the *London Gazette* of July 23 commends Lieut. Billyard-Leake 'for placing his ship by calculated manoeuvring exactly where he wanted to place her to block the canal'.

★★★★★★

According to latest reports from air observation, the two old ships, with their holds full of concrete, are lying across the canal in a V position; and it is probable that the work they set out to do has been accomplished, and that the canal is effectively blocked.

A motor-launch under Lieutenant P. T. Dean, R.N.V.R., had followed them in to bring away the crews, and waited further up the canal towards the mouth against the western bank. Lieutenant Bonham-Carter, having sent away his boats, was reduced to a Carley float, an apparatus like an exaggerated life-buoy with a floor of grating. Upon contact with the water it ignited a calcium flare, and he was adrift in the uncanny illumination with a German machine-gun a few hundred yards away giving him its undivided attention.

What saved him was possibly the fact that the defunct *Intrepid* was still emitting huge clouds of smoke which it had been worth nobody's while to turn off. He managed to catch a rope as the motor-launch started, and was towed for a while till he was observed and taken on board. Another officer jumped ashore and ran along the bank to the launch. A bullet from the machine-gun stung him as he ran, and when he arrived, charging down the bank out of the dark, he was received by a member of the launch's crew, who attacked him with a hammer.

53

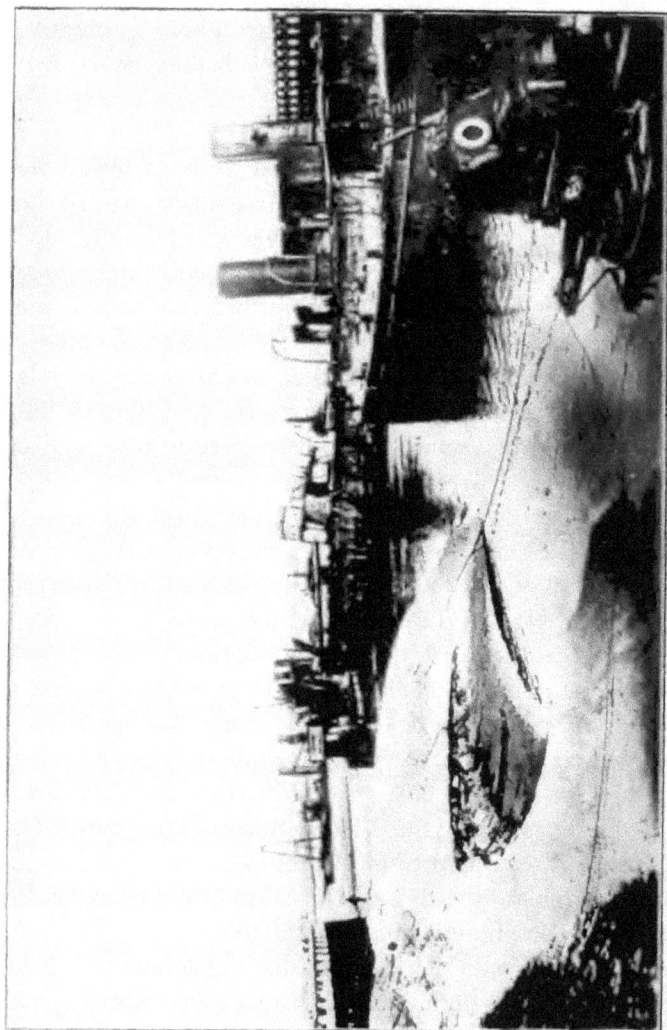

THE SUNKEN SHIPS AT ZEEBRUGGE, (SEPTEMBER 1918)

Note: The photograph was taken at low water looking out to sea between the timber piers of the Canal entrance: Mole on left of the picture.

★★★★★★

Commanding Motor-launch 282. Lieutenant Percy Thompson Dean received the V.C. 'for most conspicuous gallantry' on the occasion. Each block-ship was followed by a M.L., carrying a crew of eight to ten volunteers, to bring away survivors.

Lieutenant Bonham-Carter with two of his officers and four petty officers remained behind, after the rest of the crew had been sent away, to see that the ship was sunk properly. The seven embarked in a Carley float, paddled down the canal and across the harbour, and were picked up by Lieutenant Dean in Motor-launch 282. Of all *Intrepid's* company only one man, Stoker P. Officer H. L. Palliser, was killed. See the Dispatch, para. 95. There were 180 officers and men in the three block-ships.

A photograph taken by a German airman (*Illustrated London News*, Feb. 22, 1919) at 11 a.m. on April 23, 1918, shows *Intrepid* still emitting clouds of smoke at that hour.

★★★★★★

The whole harbour was alive with small craft. As the motor-launch cleared the canal and came forth to the incessant geysers thrown up by the shells, rescuers and rescued had a view of yet another phase of the attack. The shore end of the Mole consists of a jetty, and here an old submarine, (C3), commanded by Lieutenant R. D. Sandford, R.N., loaded with explosives, was run into the piles and touched off, her crew getting away in a boat to where the usual launch awaited them. (Lieutenant Richard Douglas Sandford, R.N. received the V.C. 'for most conspicuous gallantry' on the occasion).

Officers describe the explosion as the greatest they ever witnessed—a huge roaring spout of flame that tore the jetty in half and left a gap of over 100 ft. The claim of another launch to have sunk a torpedo-boat alongside the jetty is supported by many observers, including officers of the *Vindictive*, who had seen her mast and funnel across the Mole and noticed them disappear. (Probably a dredger sunk by *North Star*. C.M.B. 7 torpedoed a destroyer alongside the Mole. A German destroyer was sunk in the channel close to *Intrepid* and *Iphigenia* by a heavy bomb from an aircraft some days later).

Where every moment had its deed and every deed its hero, a recital of acts of valour becomes a mere catalogue. "The men were magnificent," say the officers; the men's opinion of their leaders expresses itself in the manner in which they followed them, in their cheers, in their demeanour today while they tidy up their battered ships, setting aside the inevitable souvenirs, from the bullet-torn ensigns to great chunks of Zeebrugge Mole dragged down and still hanging in the fenders of *Vindictive.*

The motor-launch from the canal cleared the end of the Mole and there beheld, trim and ready, the shape of the *Warwick,* (Vice-Admiral Keyes directed the operations from this destroyer), with the great silk flag presented to the admiral by the officers of his old ship *Centurion.* They stood up on the crowded decks of the little craft and cheered it again and again. While *Warwick* took them on board, they saw *Vindictive,* towed loose from the Mole by *Daffodil,* turn and make for home—a great black shape, with funnels gapped and leaning out of the true, flying a vast streamer of flame as her stokers worked her up—her, the almost wreck—to a final display of seventeen knots. Her forward funnel was a sieve; her decks were a dazzle of sparks: but she brought back intact the horseshoe nailed to it, which Sir Roger Keyes had presented to her commander. (*Warwick* picked up four M.L.s. The one mentioned in the text was No. 282-Lt. P. T. Dean. It had on board 101 people from *Intrepid* and *Iphigenia.* It was dangerously overloaded. See the Dispatch, para. 111).

Meantime the destroyers *North Star, Phoebe,* and *Warwick,* which guarded *Vindictive* from action by enemy destroyers while she lay beside the Mole, had their share in the battle. (See the Dispatch, para. 111-13). *North Star* (Lieutenant-Commander K. C. Helyar, R.N.) losing her way in the smoke, emerged to the light of the star-shells, and was sunk. The German *communiqué,* which, states that only a few members of the crew could be saved by them, is in this detail of an unusual accuracy; for the *Phoebe* (Lieutenant-Commander H. E, Gore-Langton, R.N.) came up under a heavy fire in time to rescue nearly all. Throughout the operation monitors and the siege guns in Flanders, manned by the Royal Marine Artillery, heavily bombarded the enemy's batteries.

★★★★★★

Lieut.-Commander Kenneth Cary Helyar, R.N., received the D.S.O.

'When we ran into the harbour,' says a member of her crew (*Daily Mail,* April 25), 'we ran out of darkness into light brighter than daylight. They got searchlights all focused on us and at point-blank range they poured stuff into us and all over us from guns big and little. Our port side was riddled from end to end, our aft funnel went, our wireless room was put out of action, and then they smashed our bow.' From Sir Roger Keyes's Dispatch, para. 112, it appears that while *Warwick* was engaged as mentioned, *North Star* lost her bearings and emerged from the smokescreen to the S. E. of the lighthouse on the Mole. She fired all her torpedoes at vessels alongside the Mole, but was sunk by heavy fire at point-blank range, presumably by the 8-in. battery east of the Canal entrance.

Lieut. -Commander Hubert E. Gore-Langton, R.N., was specially promoted to commander for services in the action.

★★★★★★

THE ATTACK ON OSTEND.

(See Commodore Lynes's Report, and the Dispatch, para. 98 ff.)

The wind that blew back the smoke-screen at Zeebrugge served us even worse at Ostend, where that and nothing else, (this is not accurate, the displacing of the Stroom Bank buoy was the major cause of failure), prevented the success of an operation ably directed by Commodore Hubert Lynes, C.M.G. (commanding the naval light forces at Dunkirk; received the C.B. for services in the action). The coastal motor-boats had lit the approaches and the ends of the piers with calcium flares, and made a smoke cloud which effectually hid the fact from the enemy. *Sirius* and *Brilliant* were already past the Stroom Bank buoy when the wind changed, revealing the arrangements to the enemy, who extinguished the flares with gunfire.

★★★★★★

Sirius (Lieut.-Commander H. N. M. Hardy, P.N.) and *Brilliant* (Commander A. E. Godsal, R.N.) were sister ships, light cruisers of the Apollo type, displacing 3,600 tons each, launched in 1890 and 1891 respectively, with an armament of two 6-inch and lesser guns.

The Stroom Bank buoy marked the channel to the harbour entrance. It had been moved some 2,400 yards east of its customary position immediately before the attack. See the Dispatch, para. 20.

Another account (*The Times*, April 27, 1918) says that *Sirius* and *Brilliant* were about two miles from their objective when the German searchlights picked them up. The ships at once came under extremely heavy fire, which included a missile known as 'flaming onions', a small incendiary shell fastened together in chains by wire which, on finding its target, winds round it and

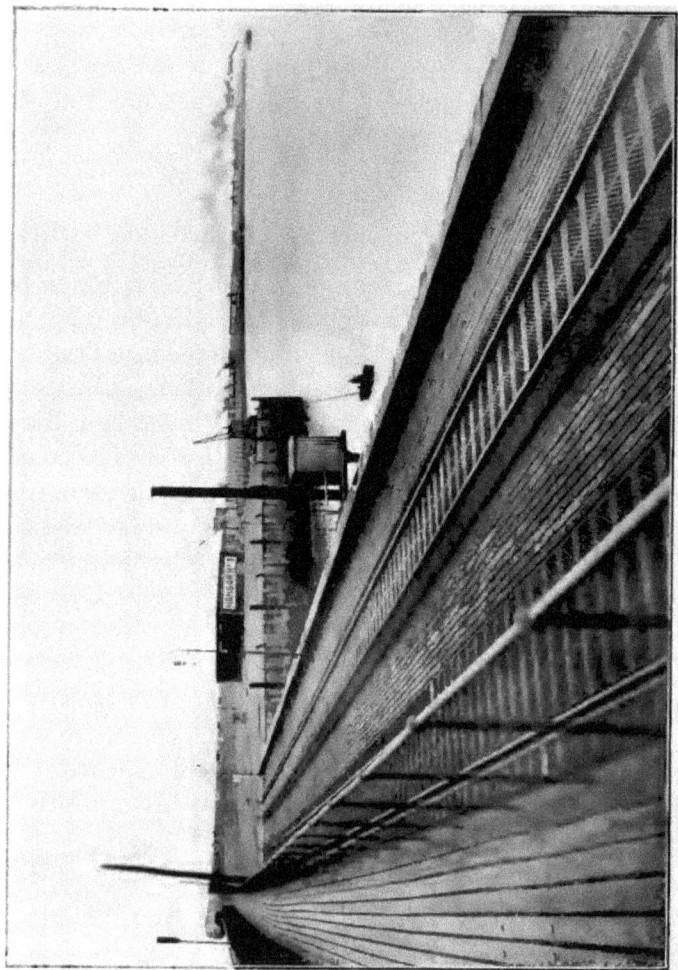

THE MOLE AT ZEEBRUGGE, SHOWING THE VIADUCT (FOREGROUND)

creates a fire. Commodore Lynes's Report (para. 11 f.) confirms this. From the Report it appears that the wind shifted about 11.50 p.m. and that the block-ships entered the smoke abreast the buoy about 12. The Dispatch, para. 26, gives 12.15 as the moment of the change of wind. The block-ships sank at 12.30 a.m.

★★★★★★

Sirius was already in a sinking condition, when at length the two ships, having failed to find the entrance, grounded and were forced, therefore, to sink themselves at a point about 400 yards east of the piers, (not correct, the exact position was 2,400 yards east of the eastern pier, see Dispatch), and their crews were taken off by motor-launches under Lieutenant K, R. Hoare, R.N.V.R., and Lieutenant R. Bourke, R.N.V.R. (M.L. 283. Lt.-Commander Keith Robin Hoare, D.S.C., R.N.V.R., received the D.S.O.; he rescued nearly all the crew of *Sirius* and sixteen of the crew of *Brilliant*. M.L. 276, Lieutenant Roland Bourke, R.N.V.R., received the D.S.O.; he rescued thirty-seven officers and men from *Brilliant*).

★★★★★★

The account quoted that the commander of *Sirius*, whose ship was sinking as the result of gunfire, tried to warn the engine-room of his intention to blow the bottom out of her. He was foiled in his purpose owing to the means of communication having been destroyed. The rush of water into the engine-room was the first indication to the staff there that the demolition charge had been fired. After leaving *Sirius* an officer and a number of men were found to be missing. A C.M.B. commanded by Acting Sub-Lieutenant Peter Booth Clarke, R.N.R, with Lieutenant-Commander Henry N. M. Hardy (of *Sirius*), R.N., and Lieutenant Edward Lyon Berthon, D.S.C., returned and boarded the ship. The missing men were subsequently picked up thirteen miles out to sea. Lieutenant Berthon received a bar to the D.S.C. Sub-Lieutenant Clarke received the D.S.C. Lieutenant-Commander Hardy was promoted to Commander, See *The Navy Eternal*, and *London Gazette* of July 23, 1918.

★★★★★★

The motor-launches here at Ostend were under the command of Commander Hamilton Benn, R.N.V.R., D.S.O, M. P., (Commander Ion H. Benn, D.S.O., M.P., R.N.V.R., specially promoted to Temporary Acting Captain; was in Motor-launch 582 in one of the most

59

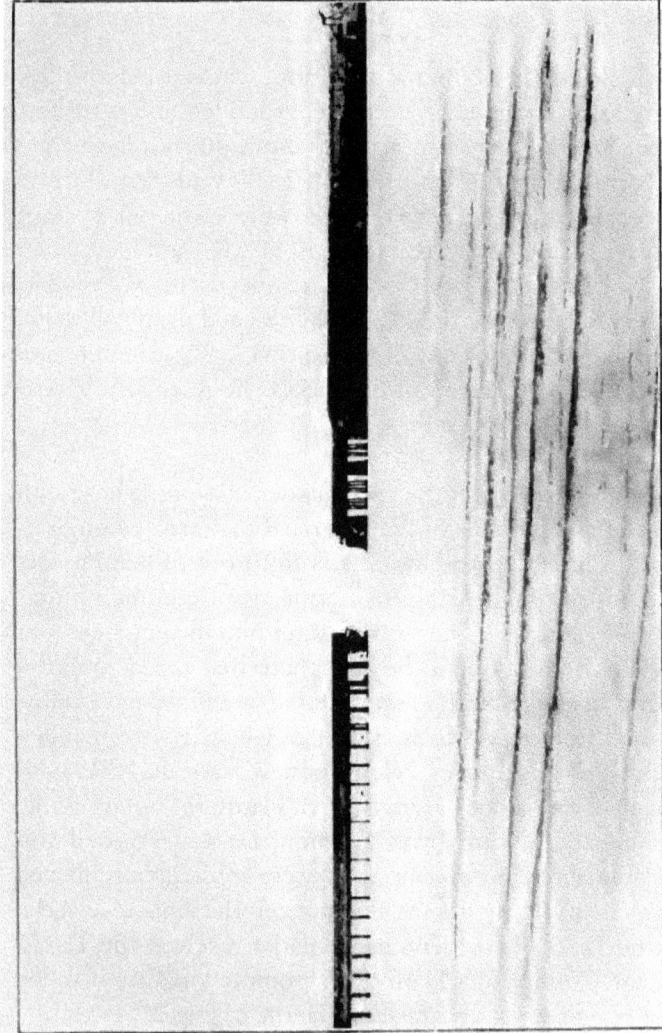

ZEEBRUGGE VIADUCT AFTER THE ATTACK

inshore berths), while those at Zeebrugge were commanded by Captain R. Collins, R.N.—the Vice-Admiral's Flag Captain—(Captain Ralph Collins, R.N., received the C.B.). All the coastal motor-boats were commanded by Lieutenant A. P. Welman, D.S.C., R.N. (Lieutenant Arthur Eric Pole Welman, D.S.C, R.N., received the D.S.O.) The torpedo-boat destroyer flotilla was commanded by Captain Wilfred Tomkinson, R.N. (received the C.B.)

The difficulty of the operation is to be gauged from the fact that from Zeebrugge to Ostend the enemy lotteries number not less than 120 heavy guns, which can concentrate on retiring ships, during daylight, up to a distance of about sixteen miles, (appears to be an understatement. See the Dispatch, para. 4). This imposes as a condition of success that the operation must be carried out at night, and not late in the night. It must take place at high water, with the wind from the right quarter, and with a calm sea for the small craft. The operation cannot be rehearsed beforehand, since the essence of it is secrecy, and though one might have to wait a long time to realise all the essential conditions of wind and weather, secrecy wears badly when large numbers of men are brought together in readiness for the attack.'

(C) THE STORMING OF ZEEBRUGGE MOLE.
(See plan following, and Dispatch, para. 67 ff.)

As has been pointed out already, the attack on Zeebrugge Mole was ancillary to the blocking of Bruges Canal, the main operation, and indeed could not be justified apart from it. There was nothing on the Mole of military importance to sanction the heavy expenditure of human life its capture would entail. But the Mole's defences had it in their power to impeach or to hamper the passage of the block-ships; it was therefore imperative that they should be put out of action before the block-ships arrived. The scheme of attack projected two almost simultaneous operations—an assault upon the Mole's batteries, particularly the three 5.9's at its sea-end, by landing parties from *Vindictive* and the Liverpool ferry-boats; and the destruction of the iron viaduct in order to close the Mole against reinforcements. The latter operation was entirely successful. The former, while it failed to destroy the seaward batteries, which opened fire again as *Vindictive* and her escort withdrew, or to do as much damage as had been intended, was effective in causing a diversion during the critical period of the block-ships' passage.

Zeebrugge Mole is a mile and a half long. The leading block-

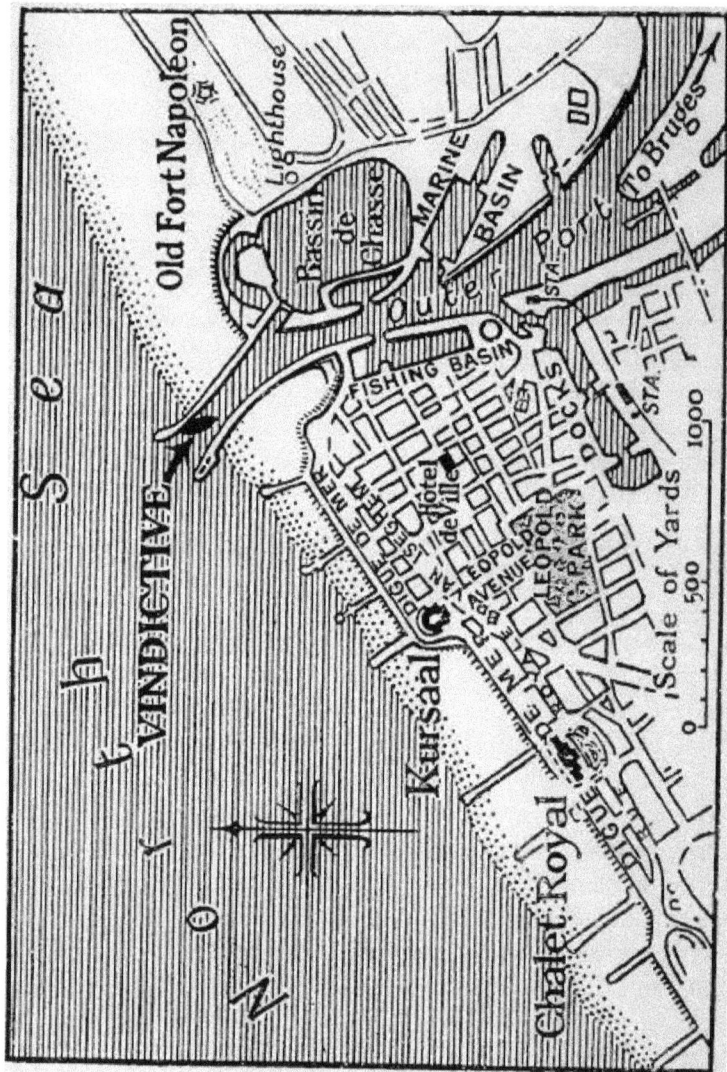

RAID ON OSTEND, MAY 10

ship, *Thetis*, was timed to pass the lighthouse twenty-five minutes after *Vindictive* got alongside. (Dispatch of May 9, para. 71). The interval was brief, and the operations on the Mole necessarily were restricted to the critical positions which menaced the block-ships' course towards the Canal piers. The most formidable of them was a battery of three 5.9 inch guns, (*ibid*), at the sea-end of the Mole proper, and the lighter guns on the Mole extension, three of which, after the evacuation, were found to be of 4.1-inch calibre, (*ibid*). The intention was to land storming parties on the top of the 5.9 battery, and to silence it and the guns on the extension before the block-ships arrived, (*ibid*). The operation was entrusted to three companies of bluejackets, under Lieutenant-Commander Arthur L. Harrison of *Lion*, (*ibid*). Captain Henry C. Halahan was in supreme command.

The second point selected for assault was a fortified zone on the Mole about 150 yards landward of the 5.9 battery, lying to the right of the berth *Vindictive* was intended to take. Its tactical position was of great importance, since it commanded the point at which *Vindictive* was planned to berth, and its guns could bear upon her landing parties as they dropped down upon the Mole. Its capture was entrusted to the Fourth Royal Marine Battalion, organised as four companies, under Lieutenant-Colonel Bertram N. Elliot, (Dispatch of May 9), and drawn from the four divisional headquarters and the Grand Fleet. It was equipped with four Stokes guns, one 11-inch howitzer, five pompoms, and Lewis guns. All the crews had been specially trained, and the howitzer crews had been put through a course at Shoeburyness, (*ibid*). Having carried the fortified zone, the marines were instructed to proceed along the Mole towards the shore and cover the operations at the sea-end against enemy troops advancing across the Viaduct. The latter's coincident destruction by submarine attack was intended to assist this result, (*ibid*).

The storming parties, having silenced the enemy's guns, were to be followed by an independent 'demolition force', whose object was to do as much damage as possible to the structures on the Mole during the transit of the block-ships to the Canal. The party was composed of a company of bluejackets, under Lieutenant Cecil C. Dickinson of *Resolution*, (received the D.S.O). Twenty-two rank-and-file of the R.M.L.I. were attached for the transport of the explosive equipment, (Dispatch, para. 69, 82).

In view of the short time available for the operation, and of the circumstances of darkness and confusion under which it would be carried out, those engaged upon it had received specialized training on a replica of the Mole, described to the men, with intentional inaccuracy, as 'a position in France'. To ensure success it was imperative that the topography made familiar to its assailants on the model should be encountered on the Mole itself; in other words, that the storming parties should land at the point where their assaults were to be delivered. Consequently, the plan was thrown out of gear by *Vindictive*, who, owing to the difficulty of recognising objects on the Mole, overran her assigned station and berthed about 400 yards nearer the shore than had been intended. It resulted that the storming parties were committed to their programme on a strange terrain, distant from the objectives for which their rehearsals had prepared them, *(ibid)*.

The outer concrete wall of the Mole, as *Vindictive* berthed beside it, rose from the sea to a height of thirty feet. Along its inner side, four feet below the top, runs a lodge or parapet eight feet wide, bounded by an iron railing, (parapet can be seen in the earlier picture). The surface of the Mole, over ninety feet wide, lies fifteen feet below it. To facilitate landing on this formidable structure *Vindictive* was provided with a false deck on the port or landing side, and eighteen landing brows or gangways to bridge the space between the false deck and the parapet. Of this number only four remained serviceable, partly owing to severe enemy gun-fire, partly to the sawing of the brows on the parapet as the vessel rocked in the swell.

The small *Iris II* was equipped with scaling ladders. She and *Daffodil* had been selected on account of their carrying capacity (1,500) and shallow draft to act as *Vindictive's* auxiliaries. (Dispatch of May 9). *Daffodil* carried two of the three parties of the demolition force, *(ibid)*. which was not required on the Mole until the storming parties had prepared for it. *Iris II* carried the Chatham Company of the storming Marines, *(ibid)*, and D Company of the naval storming party, *(ibid)*. Both vessels landed their complements over *Vindictive*, whose initial error involved their forces in the resulting confusion. *Iris's* difficulties, already narrated, also weakened both the storming and demolition operations on the Mole.

The rest of the forces were carried by *Vindictive*, and suffered much from enemy gun-fire while waiting to land. An officer writes, (*Daily Mail*, April 25, 1918):

> Perfect order prevailed. The men were lined up on deck. They fell here, there, and almost everywhere. But the instructions

64

were that those unwounded should remain in their positions, and not one moved.

The first to land were the A and B Companies of the naval storming party, under Lieutenant-Commander Bryan F. Adams, (promoted to commander), and Lieutenant G. B. T. Chamberlain, (Killed on board), respectively. They proceeded a short distance along the parapet towards the sea-end of the Mole until they reached a look-out or control station having a rangefinder behind and above it. Between it and the 5.9-inch battery, the naval storming party's objective, a machine-gun was very active about 100 yards nearer. Lieutenant-Commander Adams advanced his men to a point along the parapet forty yards east of the look-out. Here his party was protected from the machine-gun, but was exposed to the fire of the two destroyers alongside the Mole, which now began to be active.

A sortie in the direction of the machine-gun cost Lieutenant-Commander Harrison his life. The situation, in fact, was beyond the powers of a depleted force to cope with. A summons to the Marines farther westward was answered. But before their help could become effective the recall was sounded, and the storming parties fell back on *Vindictive*. Their ill-success was due to the cause already stated. But though they failed to capture the 5.9 battery, it is probable that their fire kept it out of action, for the block-ships passed unscathed by it. (Dispatch, para. 72-6. See plan).

The Marine storming party's intended objective was the fortified zone which had defeated the naval party's endeavour to reach the Mole-end battery. But as *Vindictive* berthed to landward of this zone, and as their strength was reduced by *Iris's* inability to land her detachment, the Marines turned at once to the secondary duty assigned to them—the establishment of a strong point to prevent enemy reinforcements pushing up to interfere with the work in progress at the sea-end of the Mole. They were in fact faced with a dilemma. To have attacked the fortified zone first might have given, the enemy an opening to seize positions abreast *Vindictive* and exploit them with disastrous consequences. On the other hand, unless the fortified zone was reduced, the 5.9-inch battery at the Mole-end could not be prevented from obstructing the block-ships.

The first platoon to land passed along the parapet to the right, taking a direction opposite to that followed by the naval storming party. Having silenced a body of snipers firing at the landing parties from near No. 2 Shed, the platoon reached a position some 200 yards west of *Vindictive*. Two more platoons followed and, descending to the surface of the Mole by means of rope ladders, established a strong point at the westward (shoreward) end of No. 3 Shed. Units now landed rapidly. Heavy scaling ladders were got into position, and reinforcements poured down upon the surface of the Mole to reinforce the point established near No. 3 Shed. Having secured its secondary object, the Marine force was free to dispatch reinforcements to the Naval storming party which had been brought to a standstill farther east.

In conjunction with it an attack was launched upon the fortified zone. The Marines advanced as far as the look-out station. But neither they nor the Naval storming party, some forty or fifty yards east of them, were able to make headway along the exposed parapet. The general recall interrupted the attack. The attacking force fell back in good order, the sections to the west suffering from enemy fire as they climbed to the parapet by the scaling ladders. (Dispatch, para. 77-81).

Owing to the conditions under which the storming parties worked, the demolition force's programme could not be carried out. The storming bluejackets and Marines were in such close proximity that the demolition party, for whom they had been preparing, was unable to destroy structures without endangering its own side. It was on shore for fifty-five minutes, but was only able to place charges for the destruction of No. 3 Shed in case its demolition might become practicable. An attempt to place a charge alongside the destroyers was repulsed by their fire; but bombs were thrown on board. (Dispatch, para. 82-4).

It is not surprising that the actors' accounts of a crowded and bewildering hour do little justice to its incidents and are blemished by exaggerations. After collating their statements with the Dispatch, it is necessary to discard as misleading those published in the public press on the morrow of the event.

While the storming and demolition parties were at work under baffling conditions, Sir Roger Keyes's plans were being executed with triumphant completeness at the landward end of the Mole. The object here was to prevent reinforcements passing on to the Mole across the Viaduct while the storming parties seaward were in action. The agents employed were a couple of old C class submarines—C 1 and C 3—built in 1906 and 1907 and displacing 316 tons. It was calculated that the boats, driven at a speed of six knots against the Viaduct connecting the Mole and the shore, would penetrate the light bracing of the piers up to their conning towers, a calculation exactly confirmed by the event. To enable the submarines to be abandoned at a distance and continue their course automatically, each was fitted with gyro-control, which C3's commander, Lieutenant Richard D. Sandford, disdained to use, preferring to remain on board and make sure the accomplishment of his duty. Each submarine carried two motor-skiffs and a light scaling ladder as a means of escape to the Viaduct if other equipment failed. A picket boat, commanded by Lieutenant-Commander Francis H. Sandford, was in attendance to rescue the crews if they abandoned the submarines in their motor-skiffs.

The two submarines and picket-boat approached the Mole in tow of destroyers. Owing to the parting of the tow, however, C 1 was delayed and did not reach the vicinity of the Viaduct until its destruction had been accomplished by C 3. The latter, at about a mile and a half's distance, was lit up by star-shell and became the object of a brief cannonade. At about half a mile's distance searchlights were switched on to her and were turned off again, possibly in hope that the submarine would run into the Viaduct and become a prize. At 100 yards' distance course was altered io ensure striking the Viaduct end on.

C3 struck exactly between two of the lines of piers, raised her hull bodily about two feet on to the horizontal girders, and penetrated up to the conning tower. The crew lowered the motor-skiff, whose damaged propeller compelled them to use oars. The fuses on C3 were ignited, and the skiff set off, making slow progress against the current, and under heavy fire. She was holed several times and was kept afloat only by means of a special pump. At 12.20 a.m., when the skiff was 200 or 300 yards distant, C 3 exploded, and a portion of the Viaduct was shattered to atoms. The picket-boat was sighted, and picked up the skiff's crew. Eventually *Phoebe* took them on board. (Dispatch of May 9, para. 86-91).

An officer of one of the C.M.B.s gives an account of the event, (Daily Mail, April 25, 1918): —

'The submarine (C 3) which got into position and blew up the Mole went to it from the outer side. The Huns seem to have thought that she had lost her way in the dark and that her real intention was to have gone inside the Mole in order to torpedo something. Apparently they said to themselves, "She has missed her way. Now we'll entice her in and get her."

'So they sent up star-shells in such numbers that it made the darkness just like daylight. In this way they assisted her very greatly by showing her the way to her goal. She could see them on the bridge, (*i.e.* the Viaduct), which led from the Mole to the shore. Apparently they thought that they were going to trap our submarines, and were overjoyed at the prospect. But that was really the point she was making for.

★★★★★★

'I must tell you a curious feature of this affair. As he (Sandford) approached the Mole they got the searchlights on to him and began firing at him. That was a nasty position, because she (C 3) was stuffed full of explosives, and also had a big quantity of petrol on board. But when they saw him still coming on, and dashing straight at the Mole, they stopped firing and simply gaped, I suppose they thought he was mad. Anyway, there they stood, staring at Sandford in his submarine. Then, presently, came the explosion, and bang wont the whole lot to glory!'— Statement by Captain Carpenter in Keble Howard's *The Glory of Zeebrugge.*

★★★★★★

'They pushed the submarine under this bridge and blew her up. As she was loaded with explosives you can imagine what damage she did when all this cargo went off. It blew the bridge and all the Huns standing on it right up into the air.

★★★★★★

Lieutenant Sandford, C 3's commander, states in a brief message (*Daily Mail*, April 25): 'There was no doubt about getting there, I set the fuse myself and I think the thing was done all right. Wo were lucky in being picked up by the picket-boat afterwards. The firing from the shore was a bit severe at 200 yards, and only the fact that the sea was a bit rough and we were up and down a good deal saved us. The crew did their duty, every man. They were all volunteers and picked men. We got in without difficulty and were not found by the searchlights until we were getting away.' The crew of six consisted of Lieutenant Sandford, R.N., Lieutenant J. Howell-Price, R.N, R., Coxswain W. Harner, Engine-room Artificer A. G. Roxburgh, Leading Seaman W. G. Cleaver, and Stoker H. C. Bindall.

★★★★★★

'By the blowing up of the bridge the Mole was isolated, and it was upon this island of a place that the *Vindictive* men landed and their fight with the Huns took place. And it was a rare fight too. Every one of our fellows who took part in it deserved a V.C.'

Stoker Bindall, of Submarine C 3, gives the following account, (*Daily Mail,* April 25, 1918): —

'Lieutenant Sandford commanded, with Lieutenant Price as second in command, and with her engines running smoothly the submarine glided into the shoal waters of Zeebrugge at midnight, the whole crew of six being on deck. The Mole, looming up black in the darkness, and the Viaduct joining it to the shore were clearly seen.

'It was a silent and nervy business. She was going at full tilt, when we hit the Viaduct. (At 9½ knots. Her surface speed was 14 knots). It was a good jolt, but you can stand a lot when you hang on tight. We ran right into the middle of the Viaduct and stuck there as intended. I do not think anybody said a word except "We're here all right".

'We lowered the skiff and stood by while the commander touched off the fuse. Then we tumbled into the skiff and pushed off. We had rather a bit of bad luck. The propeller fouled the exhaust-pipe and left us with only a couple of oars and two minutes to get away.

'The lights were now on us and the machine-guns going from the shore. Before we had made 200 yards the submarine went up. We had no doubt about that. There was a tremendous *flash, bang, crash,* and lots of concrete from the Mole fell all round us into the water. It was lucky we wore not struck. Coxswain Harner and I took the oars first, till I was knocked out. Then Cleaver, grabbed the oar and carried on till the coxswain was hit. I was hit again, and Lieutenant Price, lifting me and Harner into the bows, took the oar, and was afterwards relieved by Roxburgh when Lieutenant Sandford was hit. In the nick of time a picket-boat found the skiff. We gave a shout of joy when we saw her. She took us on board and transferred us to another ship.'

★★★★★★

Stoker 1st Cl. Henry Cullis Bindall, received the Conspicuous Gallantry Medal.

Leading Seaman William Gladstone Cleaver, received the Conspicuous Gallantry Medal.

Petty-Officer Walter Harner, received the Conspicuous Gallantry Medal.

Lieutenant John Howell-Price, D.S.C., R.N.R., received the D.S.O.

Engine-room Artificer Allan Gordon Roxburgh, received the

Conspicuous Gallantry Medal.

The picket-boat was commanded by Lieutenant-Commander Francis H. Sandford, D.S.O., who undertook to save his brother and crew. He was promoted to Commander.

The other ship was H.M.S. *Phoebe*, which, with Sir Roger Keyes in *Warwick* and *North Star*, had been close inshore by the Mole during the operation.

★★★★★★

The demolition of the Viaduct at 12.20 a.m. and the successful passage of the block-ships towards the Canal accomplished the purpose for which the attack upon the Mole had been organised. The programme time for retirement had not yet been reached. But *Vindictive* was only held to the Mole by *Daffodil*, and any accident to the latter would place the storming and demolition parties in grave jeopardy. *Vindictive*'s guns bearing on the Mole had been put out of action, and she herself was the target of the enemy's shore batteries. In these circumstances Captain Carpenter anticipated the vice-admiral's instructions and resolved to cast-off.

At 12.50 a.m. *Daffodil*'s siren—*Vindictive*'s having been destroyed—signalled the Mole parties to return. At 1.5 a.m. it was reported that officers and men had ceased coming on board. At 1.10 a.m. *Daffodil* began to tow *Vindictive*'s bow from the Mole. At 1.15 a.m. she was clear and got off without damage from the sea-end batteries, whose crews returned to their guns upon the retirement of the landing parties and inflicted heavy casualties upon *Iris II* as she left the Mole. She did not reach Dover until 2.45 p.m.

Vindictive, in her heroic disarray, had arrived six hours earlier. (Dispatch, para. 103-5). Sir Roger Keyes already had marked her to remedy the only serious failure in the operations of St. George's Day. For long Ostend had been of little value to the enemy, and of no value as a base. Under stress of continual bombardment, he had transferred plant and docks—except one—to Bruges, and had organised the latter as an exceedingly well-equipped base. The failure of *Sirius* and *Brilliant* on April 23 left Bruges still available for the purposes to which the enemy had adapted it.

To deny him these facilities, and to prevent his numerous craft blocked at Bruges from escaping to sea, the sealing of Ostend Harbour was essential. On May 10 Sir Roger Keyes delivered a second stroke to achieve it.

THE MOLE EXTENSION AND VIADUCT, ZEEBRUGGE

(D) The German Admiralty's Account.

Issued by the 'Chief of the Admiralty Staff of the Navy' from Berlin on April 2i, the German version of St. George's Day Raid is, as *The Times* of the following day described it, 'a fine example in the camouflage of disagreeable news':

During the night of April 22-3 an enterprise of the British naval forces against our Flanders bases, conceived on a large scale and planned regardless of sacrifice, was frustrated.

After a violent bombardment from the sea, small cruisers, escorted by numerous destroyers and motorboats, under cover of a thick veil of artificial fog, pushed forward near Ostend and Zeebrugge to quite near the coast, with the intention of destroying the locks and harbour works there. According to the statements of prisoners, a detachment of four Companies of the Royal Marines was to occupy the Mole of Zeebrugge by a *coup de main*, in order to destroy all the structures, guns, and war material on it and the vessels lying in the harbour. Only about forty of them got on the Mole. These fell into our hands, some alive, some dead. On the narrow high wall of the Mole both parties fought with the utmost fierceness.

Of the English naval forces which participated in the attack the small cruisers *Virginia* (*sic*), *Intrepid*, *Sirius* and two others of similar construction, whose names are unknown, (H.M.S. *Thetis* and *Brilliant*), were sunk close off the coast. Moreover, three torpedo-boat destroyers and a considerable number of torpedo motor-boats were sunk by our artillery fire. Only a few men of the crews could be saved by us. (See the Press Bureau account).

★★★★★★

British losses, other than the block-ships and submarine, were one destroyer (*North Star*) sunk by gunfire off the Mole, and two motor-launches (Nos. 110, 424). No other vessels were rendered unfit for further service..

★★★★★★

Beyond damage caused to the Mole by a torpedo (*sic*) hit, our harbour-works and coast batteries are quite undamaged. Of our naval forces only one torpedo-boat suffered damage of the lightest character. Our casualties are small. (One of the two destroyers alongside the Mole was torpedoed by C.M.B. 7. Another, escaping from the harbour, was hit by C.M.B. 5).

H.M.S. *Vindictive* AFTER THE RAID, SHOWING THE BROWS

CHAPTER 3

The Ostend Raid, May 10, 1918

On April 26 the Lords of the Admiralty issued an Order to the Fleet: 'Their Lordships desire to express to all ranks and ratings concerned in the recent gallant and successful enterprise on the Belgian coast their high admiration of the perfect co-operation displayed and of the single-minded determination of all to achieve their object. The disciplined daring and singular contempt of death places this exploit high in the annals of the Royal Navy and Royal Marines, and will be a proud memory of the relatives of those who fell. (The casualties were: killed, 176; wounded, 412; missing, 49, of whom 35 are believed to have been killed. Total = 637).

Admiral Fournier, sometime Minister of the French Marine, generously praised the attack on Zeebrugge as 'the finest feat of arms in the naval history of all times and all countries'. (*The Times*, May 13, 1918). 'The whole undertaking ', declared the Dutch *New Courant* of April 24, 'shows that the British Navy in nowise lacks dare-devil pluck.'

In some quarters, *e. g.* the *New York Times* of April 24, the event was greeted as 'a welcome departure inaugurating a more aggressive naval policy'. Ill-informed criticism complained that the operation ought to have been undertaken long ago, and that the Admiralty in the past had been remiss in not attempting it. The indictment indicates neglect to correlate the naval and military situations. (See article by Lieut.-Colonel Repington, *Morning Post*, April 27, 1918; Pollen, *The Navy in Battle*).

The Allies had looked forward to the campaign of 1917 to gain a decision on the Western front which should yield them possession of the Belgian coast. But the Russian collapse compelled the plans of 1917 to be completely redrafted. The prospect of an early recovery of the Flemish coast receded, and the navy, once more denied the co-operation of the army, addressed itself to render useless to the enemy ports from which there was no immediate hope of his removal. The changed military situation and not solely the substitution of active for lethargic control at the Admiralty dictated the attacks on Ostend and Zeebrugge. (See Lord Jellicoe, *The Grand Fleet*, 1914-1916).

The results achieved by the operations on April 23 proved to be more considerable than had been at first supposed. On May 9, the eve of their repetition, aerial observation established that not only was the Bruges-Zeebrugge Ship Canal blocked, but that even the lighter craft in Bruges Docks were unable to find an exit through the smaller waterways to Ostend Harbour. After April 23 at least twenty-three torpedo craft remained sealed up at Bruges. Not less than twelve sub-marines were imprisoned there also. At Zeebrugge no effective steps had been taken to clear the obstructing block-ships from the canal. (Dispatch of May 9, General Summary, para. 12).

Even in normal conditions constant dredging is needed to cope with the silt and preserve the artificial harbour against the operations of Nature which have built up the Flemish coast. But the three sunken cruisers, displacing more than 10,000 tons of water, not only impeded the process of dredging, but assisted the unceasing assault of Nature on man's handiwork. Their removal by explosive force was forbidden out of regard for the surrounding structure, and the unremitting vigi-lance of aircraft impeached the enemy from attempting to shift their position. Until Germany's evacuation of the Belgian coast in the fol-lowing autumn, the three vessels remained where their heroic crews left them. A photograph, taken at low tide from the base of the wharf on the west side of the canal, published by the Admiralty on Septem-ber 19, and reproduced in this book, proves the fact conclusively and establishes the success of the operations on St. George's Day so far as the sealing of Zeebrugge is concerned. (The Germans are reported to have endeavoured to dig the channel deeper, with a view to the obstructions becoming farther embedded).

The craft shut up at Bruges presumably were able to reach the sea by the alternative exit at Ostend. And the port, owing to the failure of *Sirius* and *Brilliant* on April 23, was still used by incoming enemy torpedo craft and submarines. The former, moreover, were reinforced by destroyers from the Bight, brought down to the Flanders coast to replace those in Bruges. (Dispatch of June 15, para. 6, 7). Hence, when he learnt, on April 23, that the attempt to block Ostend had not succeeded, Sir Roger Keyes represented to the Admiralty the desirability of repeating the operation at once. The quicker the delivery of the new attack, the greater the element of surprise and consequent probability of success. *Vindictive*, the only vessel available as a block-ship, was forthwith devoted to that service.

About four days still remained during which the coincidence of high tide and darkness at Ostend permitted the operation to be undertaken. Within that period *Vindictive* was completed at Dover. Her after magazines and upper bunkers on both sides were filled with 200 tons of wet cement, the maximum weight she could carry in view of the depth of water in the approaches to Ostend Harbour. The officers of *Sirius* and *Brilliant* begged to be employed. As Commander A. E. Godsal of *Brilliant* had led the attempt on April 23. he and his officers were chosen. *Vindictive's* old engine-room staff—Engineer Lt.-Commander William A. Bury and four artificers—pleaded their intimate knowledge of the cruiser's engines, and also were accepted on her last commission. Lieutenant Sir John Alleyne, who had been employed in refitting her navigational arrangements, was selected to navigate her. Her crew were volunteers from vessels of the Dover Patrol. (Sir Roger Keyes's Dispatch of June 15, para. 2, 3).

Vindictive was in all respects ready for sea by the desired date. But a spell of bad weather set in. Strong northerly gales raised rough seas, in which the small motor craft could not operate. The attack consequently was postponed until the necessary conjunction of high tide and darkness recurred, a period which opened on the night of May 9-10. The delay made it possible to prepare a second block-ship, the obsolescent *Sappho*, a light cruiser of the *Sirius* and *Brilliant* class, (completed in 1893; displacement 3,400 tons), whose failure she was intended to make good. She was forthwith equipped at Chatham. The officers of *Sirius* received the command, and volunteers from the Chatham Royal Naval Barracks provided her crew. (Dispatch of June 15, para. 4, 5; Commodore Lynes's Report, para. 9-11).

The enforced postponement permitted Commodore Lynes, to whom Sir Roger Keyes again entrusted the general command, to perfect the arrangements for ensuring the block-ships' certain access to their goal. Small, but important, improvements were introduced into the smoke gear, and so many alternatives were provided for guiding the block-ships to the harbour entrance that the chance of failure was reduced to the smallest dimensions. The preliminary staff-work also included precise orders for laying the smoke-screen, with plans calculated for every direction of the wind. (Press Bureau Narrative). It was necessary to assume that the enemy, instructed by his experience on April 23, would be on the alert to make counter-preparations against an exactly similar attack. While following the original scheme in its general outline, therefore, the smoke gear was improved, and the small craft were reorganised in accordance with new and alternative plans of attack. In particular, it was determined that there should be no preliminary bombardment by the monitors and Flanders batteries or by the Air Force. (Commodore Lynes, para. 5-7, 18.

The enemy, on his side, had made special preparations in anticipation of a renewed attack. (Sir Roger Keyes's Dispatch of July 24, para. 2, 3). A considerable number of his destroyers had been called down from the Bight to reinforce the crippled Flanders force. (Dispatch of June 15, para. 7). The deep-draught route from Ostend to seaward had been mined, a precaution which almost succeeded in sinking Sir Roger Keyes and his flagship, (*ibid*). Gaps had been cut in the piers as a precaution against a landing, (Press Bureau Narrative), and the buoys had been removed. On the other hand, as on April 23, the enemy's measures against surprise did not include the use of patrol craft in the offing, though nine of his destroyers were out on May 9. (Commodore Lynes, para. 12, 17).

The night of May 9-10 opened a new conjunction of darkness and high tide, and invited the postponed attack. By good fortune weather conditions on the 9th were promising, after days of rain, cloud, and mist which prevented more than the scantiest air reconnaissance. On the afternoon of the 9th, therefore, *Sappho* proceeded to Dover, whence, at 6 p.m., in company with *Vindictive* and their escorts, she steamed to Dunkirk. The cruisers anchored there after dark. Meanwhile, towards sunset, an air reconnaissance revealed the fact that the Stroom Bank buoy marking the channel into Ostend Harbour had been removed. It was arranged to replace it by a special calcic-phosphide light-buoy, a device which promised a satisfactory departure-point for the block-ships and smoke-laying craft. (The buoy was laid by H.M.S. *Faulknor*, flying the commodore's broad pennant. See Press Bureau Narrative).

As the afternoon advanced the weather conditions continued to be propitious. The wind, N. by W., blew from the right direction to carry the fog-screen ahead of the block-ships; the sea was smooth for the small craft, the sky clear, barometer steady, and atmosphere good for air observation and navigation. (Commodore Lynes, para. 11, 12, 13).

At midnight the block-ships and the small craft—M.L.s and

C.M.B.s—with the commodore in H.M.S. *Faulknor*—set out towards Ostend. Midway between Ostend and Zeebrugge a division of destroyers—H.M.S. *Warwick* flying Sir Roger Keyes's flag. *Whirlwind, Velox,* and *Trident*—cruised in order to prevent interference from Zeebrugge by the enemy destroyer force recently arrived from the Bight. (Dispatch of June 16, para. 9). Monitors took their stations out at sea ready to open fire at a signal. Squadrons of the R.A.F. attached to the Dover Patrol were detailed to bomb the port from the air, and the heavy batteries of the Royal Marine Artillery in Flanders were ready to co-operate.

At the outset an ill-timed accident threatened a further postponement. Hardly had the block -ships left Dunkirk Roads when *Sappho's* speed was reduced to about six knots by the blowing out of a man-hole joint in the side of her boiler. Her participation in the operation was out of the question. The reduction in the blocking material was serious. Commodore Lynes, however, decided to proceed with *Vindictive* alone, (Commodore Lynes, para. 11, 15), and the event justified his decision.

By 1.30 a.m. (May 10) preliminary dispositions were completed, and the C.M.B.s and M.L.s steamed inshore towards Ostend to carry out their several duties. No patrol craft were encountered, and occasional star-shells and 'flaming onions' alone indicated the enemy's alertness against surprise. At 1.35 a.m. a searchlight peered out to sea, where the C.M.B.s were already running their smoke-screens. At 1.43 a.m., seventeen minutes before *Vindictive* was due at the harbour mouth, the commodore signalled 'open fire'. Simultaneously a storm of bombs and shells from monitors, land batteries, and air-planes burst upon the enemy, while a couple of C.M.B.s raced forward and torpedoed the piers. Five minutes later (1.50 a.m.) the sky suddenly became overcast. A thick sea-fog settled down over the harbour's approaches, and for a critical hour the ships engaged in the operation kept in touch by sound alone. The fog, happily, was local. It neither reached the monitors to the westward nor prevented the airmen from continuing their attacks above it. (Commodore Lynes, para. 17-21).

Meanwhile, a heavy and continuous barrage-fire across the entrance to Ostend Harbour showed that the enemy already realised the nature of the attack. While the monitors came as close inshore as was feasible to bring their secondary armaments to bear, the offshore destroyer force was directed to fire star-shell to light up the entrance, and to pound the land batteries in order to divert their attention from the approaching block-ship. Passing at 1.39 a.m. the calcic-phosphide buoy laid by the commodore, *Vindictive* had before her a critical twenty minutes before the harbour mouth was reached. (The time is deduced from the Press Bureau Narrative, which states that *Vindictive* made the light-buoy four minutes before the signal was given to open fire).

Only half of it was traversed when the fog settled down. Punctually at 2 a.m. the old ship arrived at the point where she expected to make the entrance. Twenty minutes elapsed before she found it. Visibility was reduced to 200 or 300 yards, and nothing could be seen. (Commodore Lynes, para. 22-24).

★★★★★★

Lieutenant Crutchley's Report (Dispatch of June 15, para. 10) states that *Vindictive* proceeded for thirteen minutes after passing the light-buoy before arriving at where she expected to find the entrance. She must have reached that point at 1.52 a.m. therefore.

★★★★★★

Failing to sight the entrance, *Vindictive* altered course to the westward and reduced speed. As the entrance was still not visible, she went about to eastward and returned along the shore. Once more the goal eluded her. Again altering course to westward, the entrance at length was sighted about one cable, (200 yards), distant on the port beam. Immediately the ship came under very heavy fire from the shore batteries. Commander Godsal and his officers proceeded to the conning-tower. The signal was passed to the engine-room 'preparatory abandon ship', (Lieutenant Crutchley's Report), and her C.M.B. escort received the 'last resort'. Immediately C.M.B. No. 23 (Lieutenant the Hon. Cecil E. E. Spencer) laid and lit a million candle-power 'Dover flare' to light up the entrance, (Commander Lynes, para. 29. The Press Bureau Narrative wrongly attributes this deed to C.M.B. 22). while C.M.B. No. 25 (Lieutenant Russell H. McBean) and C.M.B. No. 26 (Lieutenant Cuthbert F. B. Bowlby) torpedoed the piers and attacked the machine-guns upon them. (Commodore Lynes, para. 24, 29).

The heavy fire to which *Vindictive* was subjected severed the communication between the conning-tower and the after control. (Press Bureau Narrative). So soon as the entrance was passed Commander Godsal went outside the conning-tower to give the necessary directions for placing the ship in her blocking position. He had just made the order 'hard-a-starboard' when a heavy shell killed him, severely wounded Lieutenant Alleyne, and left Lieutenant Crutchley to take command. (Commodore Lynes, para. 25; Lieutenant Crutchley's Report).

Commander Godsal's intention had been to ram the western pier, (*i.e.* that on his right looking forward), and, taking advantage of a strong eastward tide running through the piers, to swing the ship across the channel under port helm. But when she actually found the entrance, *Vindictive* was too close to the eastern pier to use port helm without incurring the risk of grounding broadside on. Hence the commander's order 'hard-a-starboard' a few seconds before he was killed. In the circumstances Lieutenant Crutchley promptly put the port telegraph to 'full speed astern'. But the port propeller was of little value; it had been severely damaged against the Mole. For that reason, and because the tide was strong against her starboard side, *Vindictive* failed to swing across the channel as desired. The charges were fired, and she grounded at an angle of about 25 degrees to the eastern pier, leaving a considerable channel between her stern and the western pier. (Sir Roger Keyes's Dispatch of June 15, para. 11). She sank soon after 2.49 a.m.

At 2.30 a.m., in accordance with the programme, rockets were fired from the flagship recalling the small craft. (Press Bureau Narrative). Fifteen minutes later H.M.S. *Warwick* and her attendant destroyers proceeded slowly to the westward parallel to the coast, and at 3.15 a.m. observed a signal of distress from the direction of Ostend. It proceeded from M. L. 254, conveying the greater number of *Vindictive's* rescued crew. M.L. 276 brought in three more to Dunkirk. Half an hour was exhausted in transferring the wounded from M.L. 254 to the flagship. Dawn was breaking. The tide had fallen so low that it was inexpedient to return by the route inside the shoals, by which the approach had been made, and necessary to use the deep-draught route from Ostend seaward.

At 4 a.m. H.M.S. *Warwick* struck a mine which destroyed the after part of the ship. She took a heavy list and appeared to be settling down. The wounded were transferred to *Velox*, and *Whirlwind* took the flagship in tow. *Velox* was lashed alongside to steer. Progress was slow and for three hours the destroyers were within range of the enemy's batteries. Dover was reached at 4.30 p.m. on May 10. (Dispatch of June 15, para. 12-15; Commodore Lynes, para. 28). The retirement of the Dunkirk contingent was executed without casualties or incident. (Commodore Lynes, para. 31).

(A) The Press Bureau Narrative.

(*The Times,* May 15, 1918, and *The Glory of Zeebrugge.* For the official accounts see the Dispatch of June 15 and Commodore Lynes's Report).

Dunkirk, May 11, 1918.

The *Sirius* lies in the surf some 2,000 yards east of the entrance to Ostend Harbour, which she failed so gallantly to block (on April 23); and when, in the early hours of yesterday morning (May 10), the *Vindictive* groped her way through the smoke-screen and headed for the entrance, it was as though the old fighting ship awoke and looked on. A coastal motor-boat had visited her and hung a flare in her slack and rusty rigging; and that eye of unsteady fire, paling in the blaze of the star-shells, or reddening through the drift of the smoke, watched the whole great enterprise, from the moment when it hung in doubt to its ultimate triumphant success.

The planning and execution of that success had been entrusted by the Vice-Admiral, Sir Roger Keyes, to Commodore Hubert Lynes, C.M.G., (commanding at Dunkirk, the commodore directed the operations on board H.M.S. *Faulknor*), who directed the previous attempt to block the harbour with *Sirius* and *Brilliant.* Upon that occasion a combination of unforeseen and unforeseeable conditions had fought against him, upon this, the main problem was to secure the effect of a surprise attack upon an enemy who was clearly, from his ascertained dispositions, expecting him, (on the steps taken by the enemy in anticipation of a renewed attack).

★★★★★★

Commodore Lynes's Report (para. 3) attributes his failure partly to the sudden change of wind which blew the smoke-screens across the harbour at the critical moment, chiefly to the displacement of the Stroom Bank buoy.

★★★★★★

Sirius and *Brilliant* had been baffled (on April 23) by the displacement of the Stroom Bank buoy, as mentioned, which marks the channel to the harbour entrance. But since then aerial reconnaissance, (towards sunset on May 9, see Commodore Lynes, para. 12), had established that the Germans had removed the buoy altogether, and that there were now no guiding marks of any kind. They had also cut gaps in the piers as a precaution against a landing; and, further, when towards midnight on Thursday (May 9) the ships moved from their anchorage, it was known that some nine German destroyers were out and at large upon the coast. (Dispatch of June 15, para. 7). The solution of the problem is best indicated by the chronicle of the event.

It was a night that promised well for the enterprise—nearly windless, and what little breeze stirred came from a point or so west of north; a sky of lead-blue, faintly star-dotted, and no moon; a still sea for the small craft, the motor-launches and the coastal motorboats, whose work is done close inshore. From the destroyer, (H.M.S. *Faulknor*), which served the commodore for flagship the remainder of the force was visible only as swift silhouettes of blackness, destroyers bulking like cruisers in the darkness, motor-launches like destroyers, and coastal motor-boats showing themselves as racing hillocks of foam. From Dunkirk a sudden and brief flurry of gunfire announced that German aeroplanes were about—they were actually on their way to visit Calais; and over the invisible coast of Flanders the summer-lightning of the restless artillery rose and fell monotonously. (The absence of enemy patrols in the offing in commented on by Commodore Lynes, para. 17).

"There's *Vindictive!*" The muffled seamen and marines standing by the torpedo tubes and the guns turned at that name to gaze at the great black ship, seen mistily through the streaming smoke from the destroyer's funnels, plodding silently to her goal and her end. Photographs have made familiar that high-sided profile and the tall funnels with their Zeebrugge scars, always with a background of the pier at Dover against which she lay to be fitted for her last task. Now there was added to her the environment of the night, and the sea, and the greatness and tragedy of her mission.

She receded into the night astern as the destroyer raced on to lay the light-buoy, (Commodore Lynes, para. 12), that was to be her guide, and those on board saw her no more. She passed thence into the hands of the small craft, whose mission it was to guide her, light her, and hide her in the clouds of the smoke-screen.

There was no preliminary bombardment of the harbour and the batteries as before the previous attempt; that was to be the first element in the surprise. A timetable had been laid down for every stage of the operation; and the staff-work beforehand had even included precise orders for the laying of the smoke barrage, with plans calculated for every direction of wind. The monitors, anchored in their firing positions far to seaward, awaited their signal; the great siege batteries of the Royal Marine Artillery in Flanders—among the largest guns that have ever been placed on land-mountings—stood by likewise to neutralise the big German artillery along the coast; and the airmen who were to collaborate with an aerial bombardment of the town waited somewhere in the darkness overhead. The destroyers patrolled to seaward of the small craft.

★★★★★★

Besides the Dunkirk destroyers, H.M.S. *Warwick, Velox, Whirlwind, Trident* were cruising between Zeebrugge and Ostend in order to prevent the newly arrived enemy destroyers from interfering with Commodore Lynes's force. See the Dispatch of June 15, para. 9.

★★★★★★

The *Vindictive*, always at that solemn gait of hers, found the flagship's light-buoy, (at 1.39 a.m.), and bore up for where a coastal motor-boat, commanded by Lieutenant William R. Slayter, R.N., was waiting by a calcium flare upon the old position of the Stroom Bank buoy. (The flare was hidden from the shore by the smoke-screen). Four minutes before she arrived there, and 15 minutes only before she was due at the harbour mouth, the signal for the guns to open was given. (At 1.43 a.m. G.M.T., Commodore Lynes, para. 19). Two motor-boats, under Lieutenant Dayrell-Reed, R.N.R., and Lieutenant Albert L. Poland, R.N., dashed in towards the ends of the high wooden piers and torpedoed them. (C.M.B. No. 24. Lieutenant Archibald Dayrell-Reed, D.S.O., R.N.R.; received a bar to the D.S.O. C.M.B. No. 30. Lieutenant Albert Lawrence Poland, R.N.; received the Distinguished Service Cross)

There was a machine-gun on the end of the western pier, and that vanished in the roar and the leap of flame and debris which called to the guns. Over the town a flame suddenly appeared high in air and sank slowly earthwards—the signal that the aeroplanes had seen and understood; and almost coincident with their first bombs came the first shells whooping up from the monitors at sea. The surprise part of the attack was sprung. '

The surprise, despite the Germans' watchfulness, seems to have been complete. Up till the moment when the torpedoes of the motor-boats exploded there had not been a shot from the land—only occasional routine star-shells. The motor-launches were doing their work magnificently. (They began their smoke-laying operations at 1.30 a.m. so successfully that *Vindictive* was only hit by shrapnel on her way to the harbour entrance. See Lieut. Crutchley's Report).

These pocket-warships, manned by officers and men of the Royal Naval Volunteer Reserve, are specialists at smoke production; they built to either hand of the *Vincdictive's* course the likeness of a dense sea-mist driving landward with the wind. The star-shells paled and were lost as they sank into it; the beams of the searchlights seemed to break off short upon its front. It blinded the observers of the great batteries when suddenly, upon the warning of the explosions, the guns roared into action.

There was a while of tremendous uproar. The coast about Ostend is ponderously equipped with batteries, each with its name known and identified—Tirpitz, Hindenburg, Deutschland, Cecilia, and the rest. They register from six inches up to monsters of 15-inch naval pieces in land-turrets, and the Royal Marine Artillery fights a war-long duel with them. These now opened fire into the smoke and over it at the monitors; the marines and the monitors replied; and meanwhile the aeroplanes were bombing methodically and the antiaircraft guns were searching the skies for them.

★★★★★★

A writer in *The Times* of May 11, relying on 'authoritative statements made to me this (May 10) afternoon and extracts from the report of Commodore Hubert Lynes', states that the enemy began firing 'about 1.45 a.m.' G.M.T. See Commodore Lynes, para. 22. *Vindictive* was due to arrive at the harbour entrance at 2 a.m. Enemy fire continued almost without cessation until 3 a.m.

★★★★★★

Star-shells spouted up and floated down, lighting the smoke banks with spreading green fires; and those strings of luminous green balls, which airmen call "flaming onions", soared up to lose themselves in the clouds. Through all this stridency and blaze of conflict the old *Vindictive*, still unhurrying, \vas walking the lighted waters toward the entrance.

It was then that those on the destroyers became aware that what had seemed to be merely smoke was wet and cold, that the rigging was beginning to drip, that there were no longer any stars—a sea-fog had come on. (At 1.50 a.m. G.M.T. Sec Commodore Lynes, para. 20).

The destroyers had to turn on their lights and use their sirens to keep in touch with each other; the air attack was suspended, and *Vindictive*, with some distance yet to go, found herself in gross darkness. (In fact, the fog was sufficiently low lying to permit the air attacks to continue. See Commodore Lynes, para. 21).

There were motor-boats (C.M.B.s Nos. 23, 25, 26. See Commodore Lynes, para. 29), to either side of her, escorting her to the entrance, and these were supplied with what are called "Dover flares"—enormous lights capable of illuminating square miles of sea at once. (They were of one million candle-power. See Commodore Lynes, para. 29). A "Very" pistol was fired as a signal to light these, but the fog and the smoke together were too dense for even the flares. The *Vindictive* then put her helm over and started to cruise to find the entrance. Twice in her wanderings she must have passed across it, and at her third turn, upon reaching the position at which she had first lost her way, there came a rift in the mist, and she saw the entrance clear, (at 2.20 a.m. G.M.T. See Lieut. Crutchley's Report), the piers to either side, and the opening dead ahead. (Lieutenant Crutchley says the entrance was observed about one cable's distance on the port beam). The inevitable motor-boat dashed up (No. 22, commanded by Acting Lieutenant Guy L. Cockburn, R.N.), raced on into the opening under a heavy fire, and planted a flare on the water between the piers, *Vindictive* steamed over it and on. She was in. (This is incorrect. The deed is attributed to C.M.B. No. 28. Her commander, Lieut. the Hon. Cecil E. R. Spencer, R.N., was awarded the D.S.C. See Commodore Lynes, para. 20).

The guns found her at once. She was hit every few seconds after she entered, her scarred hull broken afresh in a score of places, and her decks and upper works swept. The machine-gun on the end of the western pier had been put out of action by the motor-boat's torpedo, but from other machine-guns at the inshore ends of the pier, from a position on the front, and from machine-guns apparently firing over the eastern pier, there converged upon her a hail of lead. The after-control was demolished by a shell which killed all its occupants, including Sub-Lieutenant Angus H. Maclachlan, who was in command of it. (He was in *Brilliant* as Sub-Lieutenant in the former Raid; specially promoted to Lieutenant for his services in that action; 'mentioned' in Sir Roger Reyes's Dispatch of July 24).

Upper and lower bridges and chart-room were swept by bullets, and Commander Godsal, R.N., ordered his officers to go with him to the conning-tower. (Commander Alfred E. Godsal, D.S.O., R.N.; 'mentioned' in the Dispatch of July 24; commanded *Brilliant* on April 23. Lieutenant Sir John Meynell Alleyne, Bart., D.S.C. R.N., and Lieutenant Victor Alexander Charles Crutchley, D.S.C, R.N. The lat-

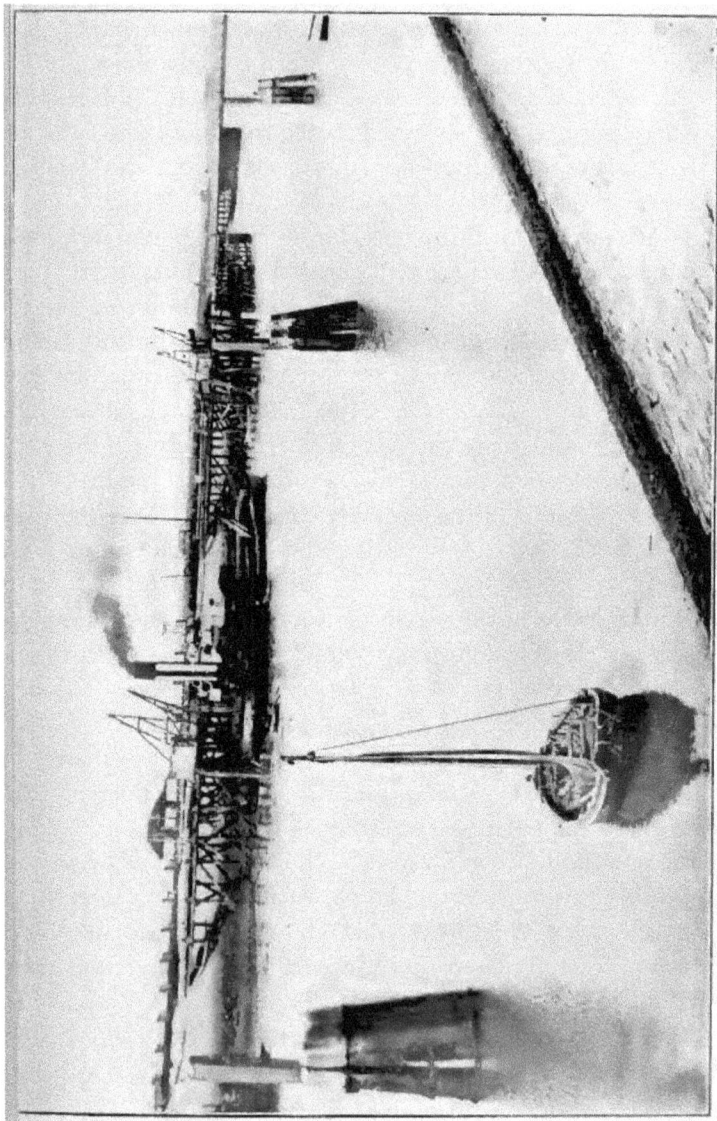

The Canal entrance Zeebrugge

ter served in *Brilliant* on April 23).

They observed through the observation slit in the steel wall of the conning-tower that the eastern pier was breached some 200 yards from its seaward end, as though at some time a ship had been in collision with it. They saw the front of the town silhouetted again and again in the light of the guns that blazed at them; the night was a patchwork of fire and darkness. Immediately after passing the breach in the pier, Commander Godsal left the conning-tower and went out on deck, the better to watch the ship's movements. He chose his position, and called in through the slit of the conning-tower his order to starboard the helm. The *Vindictive* responded; she laid her battered nose to the eastern pier, and prepared to swing her 320 feet of length across the channel. (Dispatch of June 15. para. 10, 11).

It was at that moment that a shell from the shore batteries struck the conning-tower. Lieutenant Sir John Alleyne (R.N), (received the D.S.O. Dispatch of June 15, para. 3), and Lieutenant V. A. C. Crutchley, R.N., (received the V.C. for great bravery both in *Vindictive* and M.L. 254), were still within; Commander Godsal was close to the tower outside. Lieutenant Alleyne was stunned by the shock, (he was severely wounded in the stomach); Lieutenant Crutchley shouted through the slit to the commander, and, receiving no answer, rang the port engine full speed astern to help in swinging the ship. By this time she was lying at an angle of about 40 deg. to the pier, and seemed to be hard and fast, so that it was impossible to bring her farther round. (In fact she grounded at an angle of about 25 deg. to the eastern pier. Dispatch of June 15, para. 11).

After working the engines for some minutes to no effect, Lieutenant Crutchley gave the order to clear the engine-room and abandon ship, according to the programme previously laid down. Engineer Lieutenant-Commander William A. Bury (R.N.), who was the last to leave the engine-room, blew the main charges by the switch installed aft; Lieutenant Crutchley blew the auxiliary charges in the forward 6-in. magazine from the conning-tower. (Engineer Lieutenant-Commander William Archibald Bury, R.N.; promoted to Engineer Commander and received the D.S.O. He had distinguished himself in *Vindictive* on April 23).

Those on board felt the old ship shrug as the explosive tore the bottom plates and the bulkheads from her; she sank about six feet, and lay upon the bottom of the channel. Her work was done. (According to a German account, whose chronology is reliable, *Vindictive* sank after 2.40 a.m. G.M.T. It is doubtful whether the auxiliary charges took effect. See Lieut. Crutchley's Report).

It is to be presumed that Commander Godsal was killed by the shell which struck the conning-tower. Lieutenant Crutchley, searching the ship before he left her, failed to find his body, or that of Sub-Lieutenant Maclachlan, in that wilderness of splintered wood and shattered steel. In the previous attempt to block the port, Commander Godsal had commanded *Brilliant*, and, together with all the officers of that ship and of *Sirius*, had volunteered at once for a further operation. Engineer Lieutenant-Commander Bury, who was severely wounded, had been in *Vindictive* in her attack on the Zeebrugge Mole; he had urged upon the vice-admiral his claim to remain with her, with four Engine-room Artificers, in view of his and their special knowledge of her engines. The names of these four are as follows: H. Cavanagh, H.M.S. *Vindictive*, wounded; N. Carroll, Royal Naval Barracks, Chatham, wounded; A. Thomas, H.M.S. *Lion*, missing; H. Harris, H.M.S. *Royal Sovereign*. The coxswain was First-class Petty Officer J. J. Reed, Royal Naval Barracks, Chatham, who had been with Commander Godsal in the *Brilliant*, and whose urgent request to be allowed to remain with him had been granted. The remainder of the crew were selected from a large number of volunteers from the ships of the Dover Patrol. (See the Dispatch of June 15, para. 3).

★★★★★★

Herbert Cavanagh, D.S.M.; received a bar to the D.S.M.
Norman Carroll, D.S.M.; received a bar to the D.S.M.
Alan Thomas, D.S.M., was made a prisoner of war.
Herbert Alfred Harris, D.S.M.; received a bar to the D.S.M.
P.O. Joseph James Reed, D.S.M.; received the Conspicuous Gallantry Medal.

★★★★★★

Most of the casualties were incurred while the ship was being abandoned. The men behaved with just that cheery discipline and courage which distinguished them in the Zeebrugge raid. Petty Officer Reed found Lieutenant Alleyne in the conning-tower, still unconscious, and carried him aft under a storm of fire from the machine-guns. Lieutenant Alleyne was badly hit before he could be got over the side, and fell into the water. Here he managed to catch hold of a boat-fall, and a motor-launch, (No. 276. See Commodore Lynes, para. 28), under Lieutenant Bourke, R.N.V.R., succeeded in rescuing him and two other wounded men. (Lieutenant Roland Bourke,

D.S.O., R.N.V.R.; promoted to Lieutenant-Commander and received the V.C). The remainder of the crew were taken off by Motor-launch 254, under Lieutenant Geoffrey H. Drummond, R.N.V.R., under a fierce fire. When finally, he reached the *Warwick*, the launch was practically in a sinking condition; her bows were shot to pieces.

★★★★★★

Motor-launch 254 took off Lieutenant Crutchley, Engineer Lieutenant-Commander Bury, and thirty-seven men. In all, therefore, forty-two survivors escaped from the ship.

Lieutenant Geoffrey Heneage Drummond, R.N.V.R.; promoted to Lieutenant-Commander and received the V.C. See Commodore Lynes, para, 27.

Motor-launch 254 sighted the *Warwick* at 3.15 a.m. G.M.T. See Dispatch of June 1-5, para. 10, 13.

★★★★★★

Lieutenant Drummond was himself severely wounded; his second in command, Lieutenant Gordon Ross, R.N.V.R. and one hand, were killed; a number of others were wounded. (Lieutenant Gordon F. Ross, R.N.V.R.; 'mentioned' in the Dispatch of July 24. Lieutenant Crutchley then took command. See his Report). The launch was found to be too damaged to tow, and day was breaking; she and the *Warwick* were in easy range of the forts; so, as soon as her crew and the *Vindictive's* survivors were transferred, a demolition charge was placed in her engine-room, and she was sunk.

Always according to programme, the recall rockets for the small craft were fired from the flagship at 2.30 a.m. The great red rockets whizzed up to lose themselves in the fog; they cannot have been visible half a mile away. But the work was done, and one by one the launches and motor-boats commenced to appear from the fog, stopped their engines alongside the destroyers, and exchanged news with them.

★★★★★★

Four motor-launches volunteered for rescue work inside the harbour entrance: Nos. 128 (Lieutenant-Commander Raphael Saunders, R.N.V.R.), 254 (Lieutenant G. H. Drummond, R.N.V.R.), 276 (Lieutenant Roland Bourke, R.N.V.R.), and 283 (Lieutenant-Commander Keith Robin Hoare, R.N.V.R.). The first of these commanders received the D.S.O., the second and third the V.C., and the fourth a bar to the D.S.O. Sub-Lieutenant James Petrie, R.N.V.R., who volunteered for rescue work in M. L. 276, received the D.S.C. Lieutenant Felix Francis Brayfield, R.N.V.R., who volunteered for rescue work in M. L. 128. received the D.S.C also.

★★★★★★

There were wounded men to be transferred, and dead men to be reported—their names called briefly across the water from the little swaying deck to the crowded rail above. But no one had seen a single enemy craft; the nine German destroyers who were out and free to fight had chosen the discreeter part.

★★★★★★

This is not accurate. Lieutenant Arthur E. P. Welman, D.S.O., D.S.C., R.N., encountered an enemy torpedo-boat near the entrance to Ostend. He engaged her successfully and received a bar to the D.S.O. Lieutenant William H. Bremner, R.N., received the D.S.C. for the same action. The authority already quoted (*The Times*, May 13, 1918) states that no Germans were seen on the pier. This may be so. But a very heavy fire was directed from the piers upon the C.M.B.s that torpedoed them. See Sir Roger Keyes's Dispatch of July 24.

★★★★★★

Vice-Admiral Sir Roger Keyes was present at the operation in the destroyer *Warwick* Commander Hamilton Benn, R.N.V.R, D.S.O., M.P., was in command of the motor-launches, and Lieutenant Francis C. Harrison, D.S.O., R.N., of the coastal motor-boats. The central smoke-screen was entrusted to Sub-Lieutenant Humphrey V. Low, R.N., and Sub-Lieutenant Leslie R. Blake, R.N.R. Casualties, as at present reported, stand at two officers and six men killed; two officers and ten men, all of *Vindictive*, missing, believed killed; and four officers and eight men wounded.

★★★★★★

Warwick was mined at 4 a.m. See the Dispatch of June 15, para. 12-15
Commander Ion Hamilton Benn, D.S.O., M. P., R.N.V.R.; received the C.B. and promotion to Temporary Acting Captain.
The casualties were: Officers, 2 killed, 5 wounded, 2 missing; Men, 6 killed, 9 missing. 25 wounded. Total 49.

★★★★★★

It is not claimed by the officers who carried out the operation that Ostend Harbour is completely blocked; but its purpose—to embarrass the enemy and make the harbour impracticable to any but small craft,

90

and dredging operations difficult—has been fully accomplished.'

(B) THE GERMAN ADMIRALTY'S ACCOUNT.
(*The Times*, May 11, 1918)

As on the occasion of the former Raid, the German Admiralty announced that of May 10 with characteristic effrontery.

Berlin, May 10, 1918.
At three o'clock in the morning of May 10 British naval forces, after a violent bombardment, again made a blockading attack on Ostend. Several enemy ships which, under the protection of artificial fog, tried to force their way into the harbour were driven off by the excellently directed fire of our coastal batteries. An old cruiser, entirely battered to pieces, lies aground before the harbour outside the navigation channel. The entrance into the harbour is quite free. Only dead were found on board the stranded vessel. Two survivors had sprung overboard and were captured. According to information so far received, at least two enemy motor-boats were shot away and one monitor badly damaged. (Motor-launch 254 was the only British loss) The blockading attempt has, therefore, been completely foiled. Once again the enemy sacrificed human lives and vessels in vain.'

A fuller account was transmitted through the wireless stations of the German Government two days later, (*The Times*. May 13, 1918):

Berlin, May 12, 1918.
The second attempt of the English to get at the Flanders U-boat bases, which are getting more and more troublesome to them every day, found the German Marine Corps equally prepared as on the first attempt. It could be foreseen that the English Admiralty would not be satisfied with one attempt. The reason why this time only an attack against Ostend took place cannot at the present moment be judged. It is true that simultaneously with the attack against Ostend a strong artificial mist was developed by the English before Zeebrugge, but apparently this was done only in order to effect a diversion.
In the morning of May 10 at 2.45 (1.51 a.m. G.M.T.), the enemy opened fire from the sea and from the land against the German batteries at Ostend. A few minutes later a strong ar-

tificial mist was produced. When at two minutes after three, (2.08 a.m. G.M.T.), two cruisers were sighted in the mist to the east of Ostend, the German heavy batteries immediately opened a well-directed target fire, an obstructive fire having been directed previously against the area before the entrance. (The Germans undoubtedly saw *Vindictive* twice as she sought the entrance from east to west).

One of the cruisers turned aside towards the west, the other towards the north. The latter then could be seen repeatedly in the mist and was again bombarded every time. At 3.43 a.m., (2.49 a.m. G.M.T), she loomed up again before the entrance, and, taken under the heaviest fire on all sides, sank outside the channel. In the meantime, the German batteries bombarded separate objects which could be observed at sea. A monitor, which was lying still and did not fire, and which clearly had been put out of action, was spotted at 4.13 a.m., (3.19 a.m. G.M.T.), but was immediately afterwards completely enveloped in a mist by the enemy. According to papers which have been found, the stranded cruiser is the *Vindictive*. (The 'monitor' must have been *Warwick* in her seriously damaged condition with *Velox* lashed alongside. The position is made clear in Sir Roger Keyes's Dispatch of June 15, para. 15).

The German losses, as on the occasion of the first operation, are again delightfully small.

(C) The Result

A message to Sir Roger Keyes from the War Cabinet on May 11 applauded:—

> The successful efforts you have made to deal with the submarine menace at the source. The blocking of Ostend last night puts the finishing touch to the gallant achievement at Zeebrugge.

In fact, the leader of the operations on May 10 did not regard them as final. Lieutenant Crutchley's Report to Sir Roger Keyes stated that a 'considerable channel' was still open between *Vindictive's* stern and the western pier. (Dispatch of June 15, para. 11). A postscript to the Press Bureau's Narrative therefore disclaimed the inference that Ostend Harbour was completely blocked, and a third attack was instantly planned. *Sappho's* defects were repaired at Chatham, and, with feverish haste, the old (1904) battleship *Swiftsure* was prepared as a second block-ship. The operation was fixed for the first week in June.

Meanwhile, on May 20, *The Times* announced 'on excellent authority' that the Germans had been successful in shifting *Vindictive's* position inside Ostend Harbour; that she had been swung round so that she lay through her whole length close against the eastern pier, leaving a passage of about thirty feet comparatively free for vessels to go in or out; that this left sufficient space for a destroyer of large size, though it would be difficult to get her through. (A picture of the ship as she lay when the Germans evacuated Ostend on October 17 appeared in the *Daily Mail* of October 26, 1918).

The statements are substantially correct. But Bruges, not Ostend, was aimed at. To prevent the enemy—Zeebrugge being closed—from clearing his Bruges shipping by the Ostend outlet was Sir Roger Keyes's single purpose. And aerial observation established that it had been effectually achieved by the operations on April 23 and May 10. The enemy had not contemplated the need to maintain the Ostend channels and to substitute them for the main one *via* Zeebrugge. The alternative route was wholly inadequate and the silting up of the channel made it still less practicable. At Zeebrugge also attempts to dredge a passage between *Iphigenia* and *Intrepid* were meeting with no success. The projected third attack therefore was countermanded, actually at the moment the block-ships were leaving the basin.

★★★★★★

A visitor to Zeebrugge immediately after its evacuation by the Germans on October 19, 1918, writes to *The Times* of October 30: 'The block-ships. *Intrepid* and *Iphigenia*, lie well within the piers, the latter across the passage, the other at a slight angle to the piers. *Thetis* is outside, but well across. The German torpedo-boats could only be manoeuvred past them with the greatest difficulty after extensive dredging operations had been carried out. . . . Round *Iphigenia's* conning-tower a bomb-proof shelter of reinforced concrete has been erected as a refuge for the men at work on the dredger during our air-raids.'

★★★★★★

Hence, the operations on May 10 effectually completed those of St. George's Day, and mitigated a menace to the sea communications of our army and to the sea-borne trade and food supplies of the United Kingdom which had been continual and increasing for nearly four years. (Sir Roger Keyes's Dispatch of May 9, General Summary,

93

para. 5). The blocking of Ostend and Zeebrugge, and the success of the anti-submarine barrage in the Straits of Dover, which had been carried out vigorously during the past ten months, amply supported Mr. Lloyd George's declaration to an Edinburgh audience on May 24:

> The submarine is still a menace—it is no longer a peril—as a means of inflicting injury, as a means of absorbing energies which might be better devoted to other purposes, as a means of restricting our power of transport. But as a danger which could cause the winning or losing of the war you can rule out the submarine.

Even had the operations not been crowned with success they were of precious value. At a period of tense anxiety over the situation on the Western Front in France and Flanders they braced the moral tone of the nation, which, seeing 'enshrined in the battered hull of the *Vindictive* all that had made our island home great and kept her free in a thousand years of history', (Mr. J. L. Garvin, in the Observer, Dec. 29, 1918), drank from the events a deep draught of encouragement. Mr. Lloyd George said:

> These are thrilling deeds that give new heart to a people, not merely for the hour, but, when they come to be read by our children and our children's children, for ages to come. They enrich our history, they enrich the character of our people, they fertilise the manhood of the land. (*The Times*, May 25, 1918).

Zeebrugge Affair

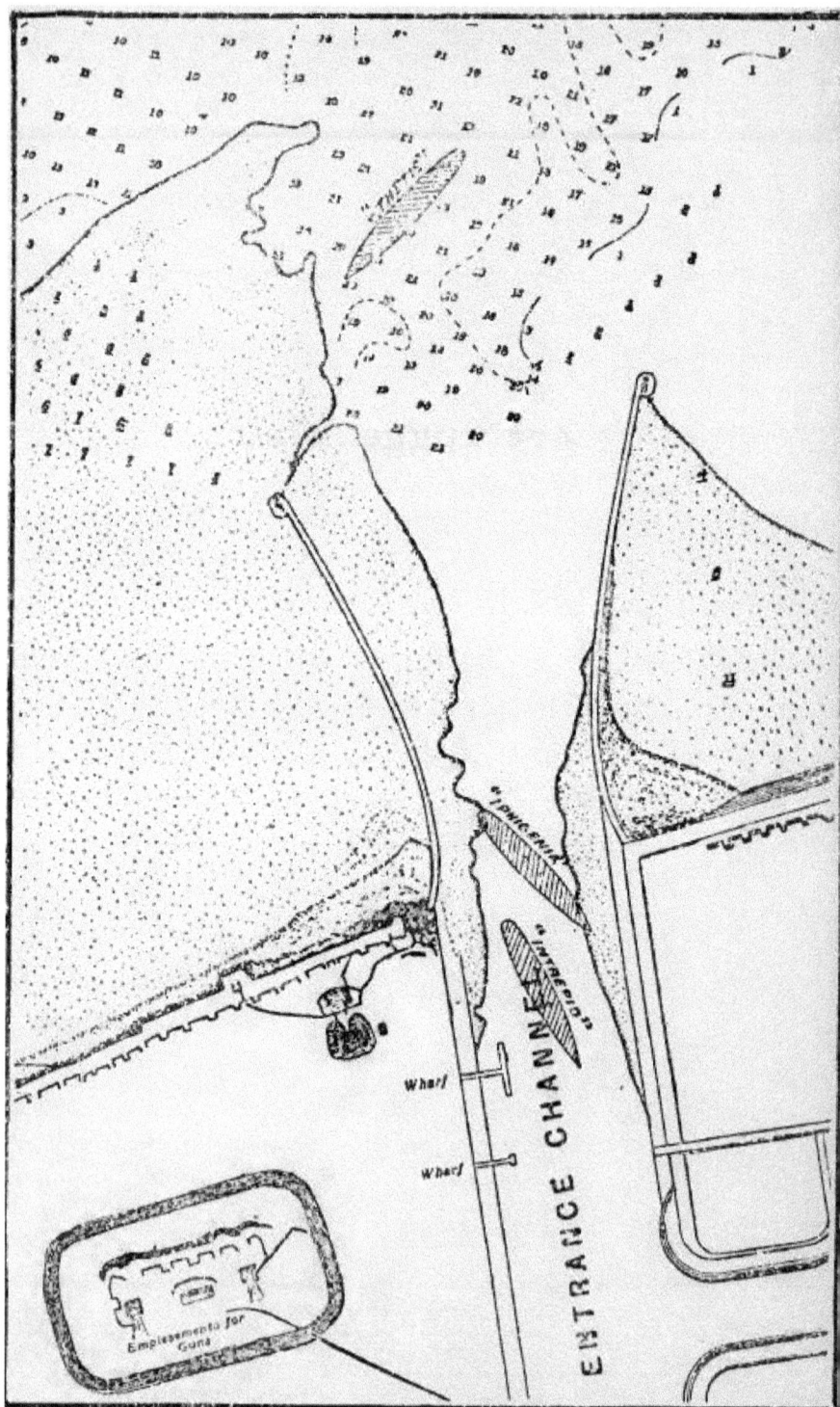

ENTRANCE CHANNEL

Wharf

Wharf

Emplacements for Guns

Contents

CHAPTER 1

What Zeebrugge and Ostend Mean

Let me, first of all, try to tell you the story of Zeebrugge as I extracted it, not without difficulty, from several of the leading spirits of that enterprise. This is no technical story. Elsewhere in this little volume you will find the official narrative issued by the Admiralty to the Press, and that contains, as all good official documents do, names, ranks, dates, times, and movements.

I lay claim to no such precision. It is my proud yet humble task to bring you face to face, if I can, with the men who went out to greet what they regarded as *certain death*—bear that in mind—in order to stop, in some measure, the German submarine menace, and to prove yet once again to all the world that the British Navy is the same in spirit as it was in the days of Nelson and far down the ages.

These men went out on the eve of St. George's Day, 1918, to do those two things—the one utilitarian, the other romantic. They went out to block the Bruges Canal at Zeebrugge—to stop that mouth which for so long past has been vomiting forth its submarines and its destroyers against our hospital ships, and our merchant vessels, and the merchant vessels of countries not engaged in this war. They blocked it so neatly, so effectively that it will be utterly useless as a submarine base for—I long to tell you the opinion of the experts, but I may not—many months to come.

This shall be proved for you as we proceed. Now let me explain, very briefly, the nature of the task which the navy set itself. You imagine Zeebrugge, perhaps, as a long and dreary breakwater, flanked by flat and sparsely populated country, with a few German coastguards dotted about, and a destroyer or two in the offing. I am certain that that is the mental picture most of us had of Zeebrugge—if we had one at all.

ADMIRAL SIR ROGER KEYES
In Command of the Operations.

Now think of Dover or Portsmouth as you knew them in times of peace. Conceive a garrison of no less than one thousand men ever on the breakwater. Glance at the plan of Zeebrugge reproduced in this book, and figure to yourself, at every possible coign of vantage, guns of mighty calibre, destroyers lurking beneath the Mole on the harbour side, searchlights at all points, and great land guns in the distance ready to pulverise any hostile craft that dares to show its nose within miles.

Picture all that as vividly as you can, and then ask yourself the question: "Would it be possible to storm Zeebrugge so successfully that block-ships could be sunk in the very mouth of the Canal and seal it up?" How would you have set about it? With a huge force of cruisers? No, for the enemy must be taken by surprise. The action must be swift, cunning, and sure. The enemy must not be warned, or your one object, the blocking of the Canal, will be lost.

It took Lord Jellicoe and Sir Rosslyn Wemyss and Sir Roger Keyes six long and anxious months to perfect their plan, with the chance that the secret, at any moment, might slip out. But it was perfect at last, and the secret had not slipped out. Next they wanted a number of men—picked men with special qualities—who would be ready and eager to die if only this amazing coup might be achieved. Last of all they wanted a night on which all the conditions—the wind, the weather, the light—should be in their favour. They did not get that, but they went in, none the less, and did the job.

We have spoken of Dover and Portsmouth. What would you say if you heard, some fine morning, that an almost obsolete German cruiser had come and leant up against the wall of Dover Harbour, that two German officers had calmly sat astride the wall in the course of their business, that some German sailors had landed on the wall and chased our gunners away from their guns, and that, in the meantime, three quite obsolete German ships, filled with concrete, had been sunk in the mouth of the harbour and blocked it? What in the world would you say?

I think you would at first refuse to believe it. Then, when some official communication lent colour to the story, you would tear your hair, declare that all was lost, and utter extremely unpleasant things about the British Forces and those in charge of them.

Yet this is precisely what happened at Zeebrugge. There is nothing more gallant in the annals of the British Navy. Not one man expected to come back. There is nothing more successful in the annals of the British Navy. They did to the full Just what they hoped and had planned to do.

CAPTAIN CARPENTER OF THE "VINDICTIVE"
WITH ONE OF THE SHIP'S MASCOTS.

CHAPTER 2

Captain Carpenter in His Attic

I cannot say that I enjoyed my journey to X———. Though representing an important Government Department, and duly accredited by his Majesty's Admiralty Office, I had misgivings. Should I find any of my heroes at X———? They were probably scattered, on leave, to the four corners of the kingdom. Or, having found a few, would they be persuaded to tell their story? Heroes, I remembered, are proverbially reticent, and it was quite possible they would smilingly refer me to the official account, offer me a cigarette, and inquire earnestly after the new piece at the Marathonium.

X——— was no longer a pleasure resort with a naval and military flavouring. It was a place of stern business. Gay dresses? There was hardly a feminine thing, if you except the sinister destroyers and twenty other varieties of war craft, to be seen. Men went their way quickly and full of purpose. That purpose may have been dinner, but even meals are short and businesslike at X——— .

The hotel—almost the only one extant—was nicely filled with heroes in embryo. The American accent fell pleasantly on the ear.

Presently my luck began. Passing through the hall after dinner, I reaped the reward of labour in the early days of the war. In those days I filled a humble position at the Admiralty, and here, advancing towards me, was an officer under whom I had, quite inefficiently, served.

To him swiftly I imparted the purpose of my mission, and by him, in the kindest way, I was conveyed back to the admiral's office. Things began to move. Gentlemen in blue and gold began to take a human as well as an official interest.

We had come to a halt outside a room on the first floor. There were two officers in the room, the door of which stood open. One was a boy. The other, whose face seemed vaguely familiar, wore the

103

The Crew of the "Vindictive" On her return from Zeebrugge

four broad gold bands that denote a captain in the Royal Navy. I studied him more closely, and noted a spare figure of medium height, a pale face, clear-cut features, and blue eyes that lit up the whole countenance with radiant intelligence. But there was something tired, too, about that face—a look that told of mental and physical strain, of days of great anxiety, of sleepless nights, and of an ordeal recently passed. Here, for a certainty, was one of my "objectives."

"Who's that?" I whispered to my guide.

"Captain Carpenter," was the answer.

"The man wvho commanded the *Vindictive?*"

"Yes. Would you like to meet him?"

"Very much."

A second—and a prodigious—stroke of luck. Captain Carpenter, one of the outstanding figures of the whole affair, was actually in X——.

Even as we conferred in whispers, however, he seemed to scent danger. With a word to the young officer, he came out of the room, ran up the next flight of stairs, and was gone. We entered the room. I repeated my little piece to the young officer.

"Oh, yes," said he. "Well, now, I wonder which people we can find for you? Nearly everybody, you see, is on leave."

"Except Captain Carpenter," I suggested.

The young officer disappeared and reappeared. He looked intensely relieved.

"Will you come up to Captain Carpenter's room?"

I floated up, and up, and up. The house was an old-fashioned one—just such a house as you will find on the front of any old-fashioned seaport town. We reached the attic—originally designed, no doubt, for a maid's bedroom. But that humble apartment is destined to become historic, for here many of the plans were drawn up that resulted in the splendid success of Zeebrugge and, later, of Ostend.

"Come in," said Captain Carpenter.

ENSIGN FLOWN BY THE "VINDICTIVE"
DURING THE ENGAGEMENT AT ZEEBRUGGE.

CHAPTER 3

How the Plans Were Laid

"Have a cigarette. Now, what can I do for you?"

I repeated my little piece.

"Well, I don't know that I can add much to the official account."

Two of my apprehensions had proved correct. But, before he could inquire earnestly after the new piece at the Marathonium, I pointed to a queer object on the floor. It was about four feet long and three feet wide. It was made of some malleable substance, and tinted a dull red. It was long, and sinuous, and decorated with tiny turrets. The base of the whole affair was painted a bluish colour. The extreme edges on the far side sagged off into a dirty brown. "What's that?" I asked abruptly.

"That? Oh, that's the Mole, you know."

"Is this the model from which they worked out the plans?"

"Yes. Does it interest you?"

"Enormously," I said.

And so it did, but the main point was that it still interested him. It was bad for him, no doubt, to have Zeebrugge on the brain after all the terrible experiences he had endured, but it was my duty to my department—possibly to a larger audience—to take advantage, if I could, of this very natural obsession.

"Then let's sit down and have a look at it."

We drew our chairs close to the model, and he began to tell me about it. It was the sailor talking, the keen navigator, the born fighter.

"Here," said Captain Carpenter, digging with his cane at the model, "is the Mole, which is eighty yards wide and about a mile long. It's divided up into portions, and you must understand that we knew all about it in peace times.

"This thin piece at the end we call the Lighthouse Pier. There are powerful searchlights, of course, at the end of that pier. Next we come

107

Official Sea-Plane photograph of Bruges showing torpedo-boats, torpedo-boat destroyers and submarines "bottled up"

to the end of the Mole proper, where we knew they had at least three very big guns. Coming along towards the land we have two sheds, one containing naval stores. So the Mole goes on in a curve until we get to the viaduct. That's the thing we blew up with the submarine. It connects the Mole with the shore end, and took an immense time to build on account of the strong current."

"Why," I asked, "did they have a viaduct? Why not have built the Mole solid all the way along?"

"Because of the silt in the harbour. They found that unless they allowed for the flow of the tide—I'm talking, of course, of when Zeebrugge was built, long before the war—they could not prevent the harbour from silting up, which, however they might dredge, would soon have blocked the entrance to the Canal. So they made that viaduct. It took, as I say, an unconscionable time to construct, even under peace conditions. There were railway lines across it, and so on. Now it's in ruins, and they'll have the pleasant job of reconstructing it, if they can, under showers of bombs from our aeroplanes.

"Well, now, here is the entrance to the Bruges Canal. That, also, was tremendously strongly fortified with big guns and searchlights. There were also guns along the banks of the Canal, and very powerful guns protecting the whole harbour from the shore. Then you must take into account the destroyers lying in the harbour. There were also some of those. We sank one. Just lobbed things over the Mole and sank it. No doubt whatever about that.

"Our job, however, was to block that Canal."

"Just a moment. Would you say that Zeebrugge was as strongly fortified as X——?"

"It was as strongly fortified," he replied, "as the Germans could fortify it, and they know something about fortification. The strength of the garrison was never less than a thousand men."

"How long did it take to make the plans?"

"We began last November, and we were at it all the time until the thing came off. I was at the Admiralty when the work started, after three and a half years with the Fleet."

"Then you practically came from a desk at the Admiralty to take command of the *Vindictive?*"

"Yes, thanks to Sir Roger Keyes, one of the finest and most gallant men that ever breathed. Not a man under him that wouldn't cut off his right hand for him. He'd have been in this up to the neck if he'd been allowed to take the risk. But that wouldn't have done, of course.

109

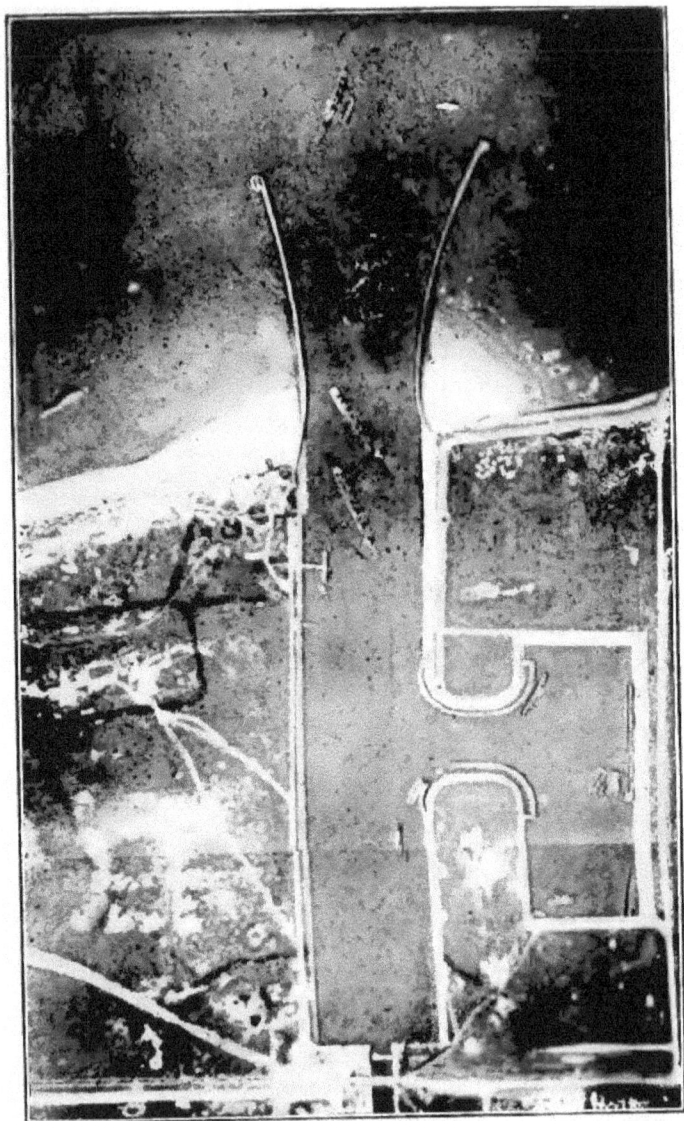

OFFICIAL SEA-PLANE PHOTOGRAPH OF THE LOCK-GATES
AND THE APPROACH TO THE LOCK AT ZEEBRUGGE, SHOWING
THE SUNKEN BLOCK-SHIPS.

He had to be in charge of the whole operation. So he very kindly told me I might command the *Vindictive*." His eyes shone with gratitude for the chance.

'There must have been a terrific lot of preliminary work!"

Captain Carpenter opened a drawer and pulled out a huge bundle of typewritten matter. "Those are the instructions," he said. "Some of them were drawn up in this room. This is where Captain Halahan and I used to work."

I remembered that Captain Halahan was one of the first killed after the *Vindictive* came alongside the Mole, and I looked at the plain wooden desk in the little attic where he had sat so many nights and worked so eagerly at the great scheme.

"Yes," said Captain Carpenter thoughtfully, but without a trace of sentimentality—he was tenderly smiling, indeed, as he thought of his friend—"he went early, and so did a good many other fine chaps, but I don't think they'd mind that. None of us expected to come back."

"How did you select the men?"

"Oh, they were all picked men—picked from volunteers. We tried them out under intensive training until we got exactly the men we wanted. That, naturally, was a long and anxious job. At first they thought it was for a hazardous operation in France, and they were keen enough then; but later, when we entrusted them with the real secret, and they knew we were after Zeebrugge and Ostend, there was no holding them! Keenness is not the word for it! They were amazing! And didn't they behave splendidly! Every man! Every single man! By Jove, one can't say too much about the way those fellows did their jobs!"

"I read in the official account that there were two previous attempts."

"Yes. We actually started twice—the whole lot of us—the old *Vindictive*, the *Daffodil*, the *Iris*, the block-ships, the smoke-boats, the motor-launches, the monitors, and the destroyers. Once we got within fifteen miles of Zeebrugge and then had to turn back."

"Rather a blow!"

"Oh, rotten, of course. We were all strung up to it, but the conditions weren't what we wanted, and the Admiral wouldn't risk failure. It really wanted more pluck on his part to turn back than to go on. It was so easy for anyone to say he'd funked it. Not that he'd care twopence for that!"

"But the night came at last!"

"Yes, it came at last. Even then the conditions weren't perfect. It was touch and go whether we started. We wanted low visibility, you see, but it was a very clear day. Still, if we waited for absolutely perfect conditions, we should never go at all. All right,' said the admiral; 'off you go.' And oft we went."

THE WRECKED BRIDGE OF THE "IRIS"

CHAPTER 4

The Great Fight

"Some people," said Captain Carpenter, "have called this affair audacious. That isn't the word I should use for it."

"What word would you use?"

"Impertinent," he replied, laughingly. "Just imagine this Armada of smoke-boats, motor launches, ferry-boats, obsolete submarines, and ancient cruisers laden with concrete, headed by the old *Vindictive*, setting out in broad daylight to attack the mighty fortress of Zeebrugge."

"In broad daylight!" I exclaimed.

"Certainly. We timed ourselves to reach the Mole by midnight, so, owing to our slow speed, we had to do three hours of the oversea passage in daylight."

"How were the men? Excited?"

"Oh, no; quite calm, and immensely relieved to be at it at last. Well, so soon as it got dark, it was dark! We could hardly see a thing, and when the smoke-boats got to work, pouring out great waves of dense smoke at regular intervals, which the light north-east wind carried right across the Mole and the harbour, pitch doesn't describe it!"

"What about the minefield?"

"H'm! Anyway, we dodged it. My job, you understand, was to get alongside the Mole, land my marines, help *Iris* and *Daffodil* to do the same, stay there drawing the fire of the batteries and diverting attention while the block-ships got into the Canal and sunk themselves, then get the marines back on board, shove off, and clear out as quickly as possible. Incidentally, of course, we meant to put out of action as many Huns as was convenient by fire from our guns. You've seen the picture of the fighting-top? That was filled with marines armed with Lewis guns. They did capital work. I'll come to that later.

"We got pretty near the Mole before they saw us, and then the fun

OFFICIAL SEA-PLANE PHOTOGRAPH OF THE VIADUCT
Destroyed by Lieut.Commander Sandford showing the
Serious Gap and the Temporary Planking.

began! Up went the star-shells, the guns began blazing, and we went pell-mell for the old Mole like that." A savage dig at the model with his cane. "I had intended to fetch up just here"—he indicated a spot on the exterior of the great wall pretty near the head of it—"but actually came in here"—a little further inland.

"We'd had things called 'brows' constructed—a sort of light drawbridge with a hinge in the middle. These were lowered away, but the current was so strong against the Mole, and the *Vindictive* bounced up and down so nimbly, that the men had the devil of a job to drop the ends of these brows on the wall.

"All this time, naturally enough, the Huns were blazing at us with everything they'd got. If you have a look at the *Vindictive* in the morning, you'll soon see what they were doing to us. We were just swept with fire from two sides. Even before the party could begin to land, Colonel Elliot and Captain Halahan, poor chaps, who were in charge of that part of the business, were killed.

'The *Iris* went ahead of me and came alongside the Mole just here"—a little nearer the shore end. "They tried to hang on with their grapnels, but couldn't quite manage it, so Lieut.-Commander Bradford and Lieut. Hawkins scrambled ashore and sat on the parapet, trying to fix the grapnels. They were both killed. . . .

"In the meantime, owing to the difficulty of securing to the Mole when alongside, I ordered the *Daffodil* to continue pushing, according to plan, so as to keep us in position. This was a pity, because she was full of men, and they couldn't land to help with the fighting. Eventually, some of them scrambled across the *Vindictive* and landed that way.

"The wind had changed about fifteen minutes before we came alongside the Mole; all the smoke had cleared off and the harbour was plain to the eye. That helped the Huns to pot at us, and they took fine advantage of it. The din, as you can guess, was terrific, and I think they got the old *Vindictive* in every visible spot.

"Suddenly the thing happened for which we had been, semi-consciously, waiting. There was a tremendous roar, and up went a huge tower of flame and debris and bodies into the black sky! My fellows cheered like mad, for they knew what it meant. Sandford had got home beneath the viaduct with his ancient submarine and touched her off. I never saw such a column of flame! It seemed a mile high!

"I must tell you a curious feature of this affair. As he approached the Mole they got the searchlights on to him and began firing at him. That was a nasty position, because she was stuffed full of explosives,

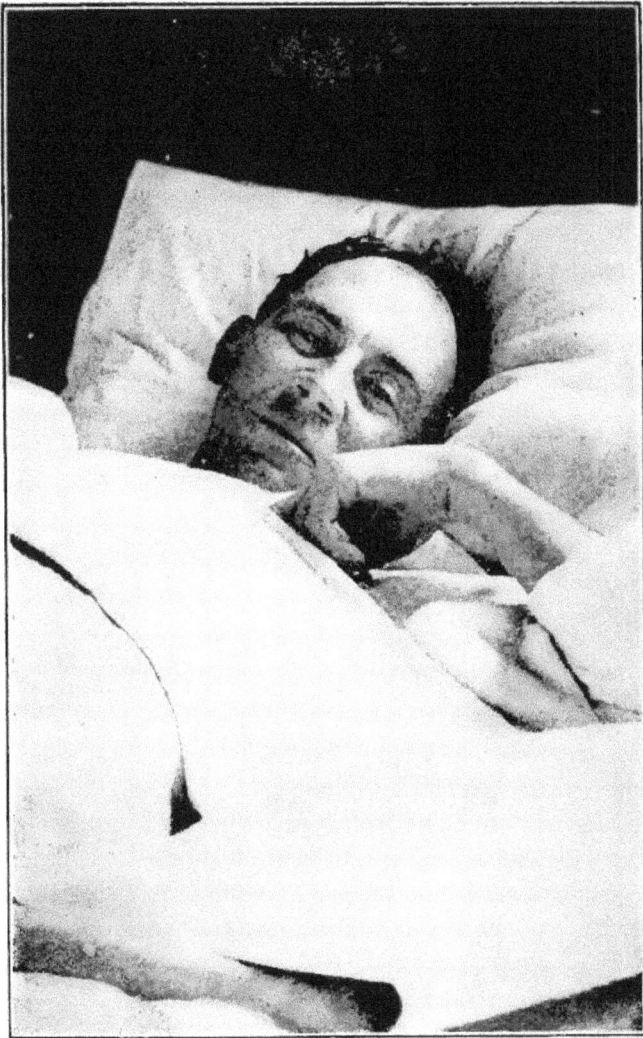

LIEUT.-COMMANDER SANDFORD
The Hero of the Submarine Exploit,
recovering from his Injuries.

and also had a big quantity of petrol on board. But when they saw him still coming on, and dashing straight at the Mole, they stopped firing and simply gaped. I suppose they thought he was mad.

"Anyway, they paid for their curiosity. On the viaduct itself there were a whole lot of Huns—masses of them. There they stood, staring at Sandford in his submarine. The searchlights lit them up. Then, presently, came the explosion, and *bang* went the whole lot to glory! They must have been the most surprised Huns since the war started.

"All this time, of course, a lot of other things were happening. Many of the seamen and Marines had landed on the Mole and were making fine play with the astonished Germans. Some went right to the head of the Mole and found the guns deserted. One gun, I must tell you, had not even been uncovered, which is clear proof that the garrison was taken by surprise. Others were chasing the enemy all down the Mole towards the viaduct, which they were never to cross, and some went into the shed I told you about and dealt with such people as they found.

"The men in the fighting-top were also doing fell work. All along the Mole, you see, and close under the fifteen-foot parapet, there are dug-outs or funk-holes. At first the Huns popped into these, but by-and-by it occurred to them that they would certainly be found and spitted if they stayed there, so the bright idea occurred to them of nipping across the Mole and dropping down the side into their own destroyers lying there. An excellent scheme but for our fellows in the fighting-top, who picked them off with their Lewis guns as they ran.

"Those chaps in the fighting-top had to pay for it, though, in the end. They were attracting a lot of attention, and the Huns were constantly trying to drop a shell amongst them. They succeeded at last, I'm sorry to say, and laid out every man jack but one—Sergeant Finch. He was wounded badly, but dragged himself out from under the bodies of his pals and went on working his little gun until he couldn't work it any longer.

"Now we come to the block-ships. We saw *Thetis* come steaming into the harbour in grand style. She made straight for the opening to the Canal, and you can imagine that she was a blaze of light and a target for every big thing they could bring to bear. She was going toppingly, all the same, when she had the rotten luck to catch her propeller in the defence-nets. Even then, however, she did fine work. She signalled instructions to the *Intrepid* and *Iphigenia*, and so they managed to avoid the nets. It was a gorgeous piece of co-operation!

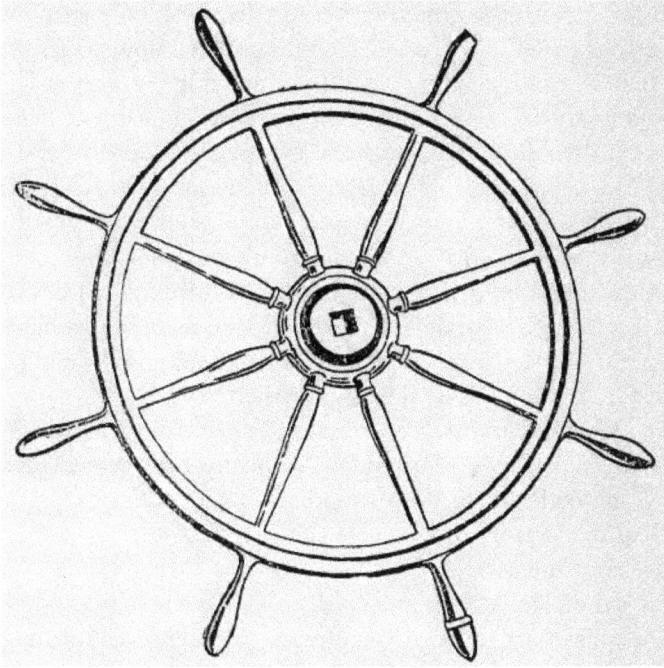

THE STEERING-WHEEL OF H.M.S. *VINDICTIVE*.

"And, by the way, I'm not at all sure that *Thetis* won't give even more trouble to the enemy than the other two. I told you something, I think, about the tendency of the harbour to silt up. Well, *Thetis* is lying plump in the channel that must always be kept clear of silt. The consequence is that the silt will collect all round her and over her, and I doubt whether she will ever be removable.

"To get back to the other block-ships. In went *Intrepid*, and in after her went *Iphigenia*. They weren't content, you know, to sink themselves at the mouth of the Canal. That was not the idea at all. They had to go right in, with guns firing point-blank at them from both banks, sink their ships, and get back as best they could. And they did it. They blocked that Canal as neatly and effectively as we could have wished in our most optimistic moments, and then, thanks to the little motor-launches, which were handled with the finest skill and pluck, the commanders and men got back to safety. Tomorrow I'll show you some aeroplane photographs which are due in from France, and you'll see for yourself how beautifully *Intrepid* and *Iphigenia* are lying."

"And how long will it take to clear them away?"

"We've had the opinion of the most expert salvagemen from Liverpool, and they say —— months. Personally, I'm prepared to swear that it won't be less than —— months."

"What may I say?"

"Say 'some' months."

"Can't they blow them up?"

"Not a bit of it. How can you blow up a thing that's already blown up?"

"I don't know. Let's get back to the fight."

"Right. As soon as we saw that the block-ships were sunk we knew that our job was done. Now came the most ticklish part of the business—to get away. Up to this point we had been protected, so far as our hull was concerned, by the Mole. We knew that, directly we left the Mole, we should be in for it.

"The signal arranged for the men to re-embark was a long blast from *Vindictive's* siren. But that had gone with a lot of other tackle, so we did the best we could with *Daffodil's* little hooter. (Ferry passengers across the Mersey must know it well.) It wasn't much of a hoot, but the fellows heard it, and made for the scaling-ladders.

"This was the Hun's chance. The fire turned on those chaps as they chambered up the ladders, most of them trying to carry a dead or wounded pal, was awful. Talk about heroism! Every man was a hero!

THE FERRY-BOATS *IRIS* AND *DAFFODIL*

You must ask some of them who actually landed to tell you about that. Wonderful!

"We got them aboard at last, and stayed to make certain that nobody was left behind. Then we shoved off from the Mole, which had had enough of us for one night, and made for home at our best speed. Instantly the big shore-guns and everything else vicious blazed away, but the very wind which had turned against us when we arrived now stood our friend. We worked all our smoke-boxes like mad, and the smoke saved us. They landed some shells home, of course, and a lot of poor fellows in the *Iris* were killed by one shell just as they were leaving the Mole. But most of the stuff aimed at the *Vindictive* fell short, thank God, and we finally ran out of range.

"It was a good fight. I think the Huns had the wind up that night.
. . .

"Where are you staying? . . . Good. So am I. We'll walk along together."

VIEW OF THE "VINDICTIVE" AFTER HER RETURN
Showing improvised brows used for landing at Zeebrugge

Chapter 5

A Museum in a Trunk

The clocks of X—— were pointing to midnight when we came down from Captain Carpenter's little office under the roof. The night was dark, but out to sea there were strange lights which boded ill, one felt, to hostile and inquisitive strangers.

We had been talking for about an hour—or, rather, Captain Carpenter had been patiently explaining the details of the attack, adapting his terms to the intelligence of a mere landsman. Anyway, I know that my head ached with the concentrated excitement of it all, and we both grasped eagerly at the two last bottles of ginger ale from the night porter's store.

"Incidentally," I remarked, "you have told me nothing at all of your own experiences and sensations."

"Oh," he laughed, "they were so confused that I couldn't possibly analyse them. I know there was the very devil of a row, and vast quantities of smoke, and all that sort of thing."

"I don't quite understand how it was that you, personally, were not killed."

"Neither do I. It's a trite phrase, I know, but I must have had a charmed life. Fellows on each side of me were cut to bits with bursting shells. Yet I got nothing worse than a flesh wound in the shoulder from a fragment of shell."

"By the way," I observed, "I read somewhere that you actually brought away a huge piece of the Mole on the deck of the *Vindictive*?"

"Quite right. Like to see a bit of it?"

"Tomorrow?"

"Tonight, if you like. I've got some up in my bedroom."

Thus it happened that we went up in the lift to have a look at the Mole, There was a trunk at the foot of the captain's bed. Unlocking this, he produced a large lump of crumbly substance and placed it in my hands. I had heard of people chipping fragments off Shakespeare's house and Canterbury Cathedral, but this went one better.

"Yes. I think you were right in using the word 'impertinence.'"

He wrapped the fragment in cotton-wool, explaining that it crumbled so very easily and was intended as a gift. The huge block that fell on the deck of the *Vindictive* was to be divided up. Sir Roger Keyes, of course, would claim a share, and the Lords of the Admiralty, but the main bulk he had decided to present to the War Museum in London, for memorial purposes.

I was still peering into the trunk. A miscellaneous jumble met the eye—a cap, a flag, a leather case for binoculars, two pairs of goggles, a broken watch (or was it a chronometer?), and a roll of tattered charts.

"Don't shut it for a moment," I begged. "Are these more souvenirs?"

"Well, just one or two little things of personal interest. Care to see 'em?"

"If you don't mind showing them."

"That's the cap I was wearing at the time. It's rather a shabby old thing, but I thought it hardly worthwhile to put on a good cap for a job of that sort. Good thing I didn't."

It had been perforated from back to front and from side to side with bullets. In each case the bullet quite obviously missed the scalp by the fraction of an inch.

"Just as well," I agreed. "Pity to waste a really good cap on a place like Zeebrugge. You were evidently there. What happened to the binocular case?"

"Well, that's rather interesting. I had my glasses in my hand most of the time, so far as I remember, and the leather case, of course, was slung at my back. A bullet went right through it, and yet I knew nothing at all about it. Wasn't that rum?"

'The gods apparently want you on earth a little longer. The barometer went as well, I observe."

"It did. All in bits. I don't know how or when. Oh, here are the old charts." He unrolled three large charts that looked as if rats had been feeding on them for six months. From each chart huge pieces had entirely disappeared, and what was left looked particularly mangy.

Captain Carpenter called my attention to the chart of Zeebrugge.

"We had mapped out three courses, you see, to allow for the wind and tide. Eventually we came round here, and the tide carried us alongside the Mole—there. Sorry they're in such a rotten state, but the chart-house was a nasty mess. Quite chawed up."

Last of all he showed me the flag—the glorious ensign—blackened with smoke and considerably holed. "We kept it flying all the time," he explained. "We thought we might as well."

I gazed at it—as many thousands of people will gaze at it when it finds a suitable home—in reverence. Then, the hour being nearly one o'clock, I took a grateful and respectful leave.

"See you in the morning," said the captain. "I breakfast about eight-thirty. You've got to look at those aeroplane photographs, and then we'll send you off in a car to inspect the *Vindictive*. Goodnight."

At my last glimpse of him, he was bundling his priceless souvenirs back into the trunk at the foot of his bed.

CHAPTER 6

On Board H.M.S. "Vindictive"

We returned next morning to the admiral's office, and I was presently staring through a powerful glass at the aeroplane photographs of the sunken block-ships. Unless you are accustomed to studying photographs taken from aeroplanes, they are at first a little puzzling, but I soon made out the *Intrepid* and *Iphigenia* quite clearly. The former was lying almost dead across the narrow channel, and had heeled over. Her nose rested on the mud-bank one side, and her stern on the mud-bank on the other side. As for the *Iphigenia*, she lay bang across the bed of the Canal. Both ships, in short, were in such a position that nothing much heavier than a cork could possibly pass them.

I have laid stress upon this, because so many people have asked, "Did the expedition succeed? Is the Canal blocked?" I can certify that the expedition did succeed, and that the Canal is utterly and completely blocked.

I now hopped into the Staff Car (with an acute sense of my unworthiness), and, accompanied by a commander and a lieutenant, who were all that the historic courtesy of the navy could lead one to expect, went off to view the remains of the *Vindictive*.

I say "remains" advisedly, for no ship that had withstood for one solid hour that fearful bombardment could hope to return anything else but a wreck, if she returned at all.

The great shell-torn funnels first caught the eye, with the smoke even then pouring out at a hundred holes. Next one noticed the famous "brows," one or two intact, others splintered. The false deck, built to enable the storming party to gain the Mole, was still in position, lined with protective sandbags. I saw the ruined chart-house, and the shell-torn bridge, and the specially constructed flame-throwing huts.

Men swarmed everywhere, trying (as I then thought) to restore chaos to order. And one was struck with the apparent hopelessness of it all. The old ship had done her job, and might, one felt, be allowed to rest in peace—perhaps alongside the *Victory*. But, as we now know, there was a far greater end in store for her!

Peculiarly interesting was the fighting-top—a circular nest high above the bridge. Here it was that the marines with the Lewis guns were stationed. One pictured that tiny fortress filled with men, every man a picked shot. Suddenly comes the crash of the enemy shell—a lucky shot that penetrates the armour of the fighting-top and lays low every man but one. The story of that man has been already touched upon. An hour later I was by his bedside in a hospital some miles away.

Yes, you had only to look at the *Vindictive* to realise what that night attack on Zeebrugge really meant. You could picture the landing-parties dashing across those narrow, oscillating "brows" on to the parapet, whence they must drop sixteen feet before getting to grips with the enemy. And you could picture the return of the grimy survivors, each man with a pal in his arms.

You could picture the decks strewn with the dead and wounded. You could see brave men, mortally hurt, raising themselves in agony to cheer on their comrades as they rushed to the battle. You could see the gunners, and the firemen, and the gallant fellows who were there to work the rockets and the smokeboxes.

Finally, you could see the pale, eager face of the commander, now on the bridge, now visiting the wounded, now issuing directions through his megaphone to the tiny attendant ferry-boats. And all the while the guns roar, and the shells shriek and crash, and the bullets hail on the dead and on the living.

"Bit knocked about, isn't she?" said the commander.

"Rather a mess," I agreed.

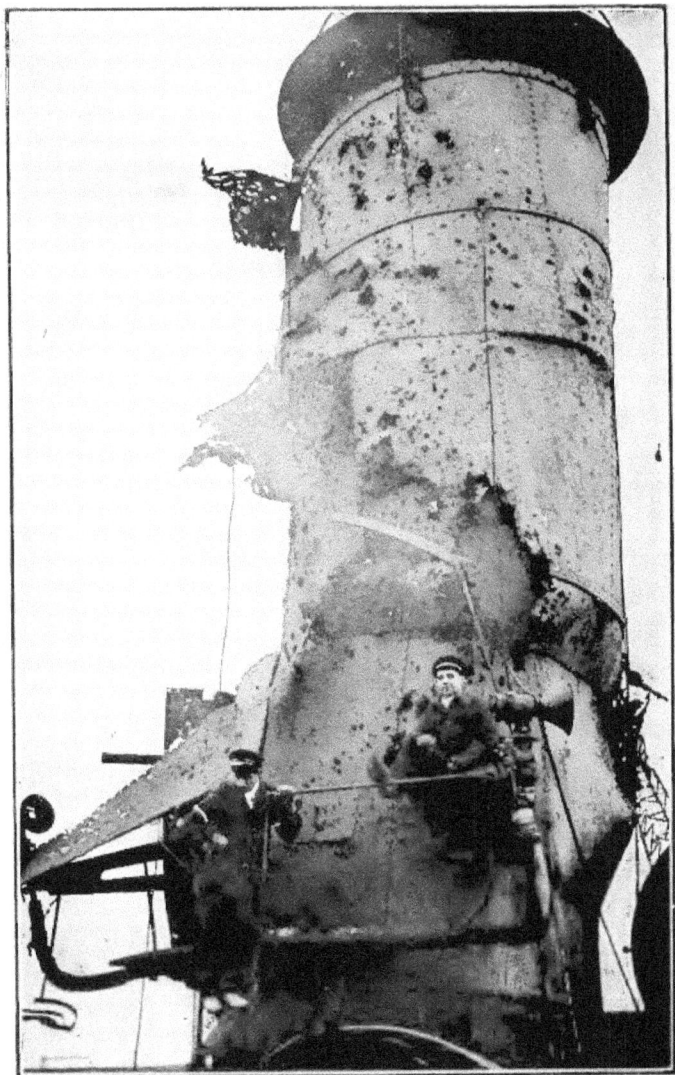

One of the Funnels of the "Vindictive"
after the Engagement.

CHAPTER 7

The Man Who Felt Frightened

It was a military atmosphere into which I was plunged at Y———. The marines, whose gallant share in the Zeebrugge exploit ranks equal to that of the navy, and will never be forgotten, were ready for me. I was taken first of all to the office of Major Carpenter—a cousin, oddly enough, of Captain Carpenter, R.N.

"Now," said he, "one of the men I want you to see is Captain Arthur Chater. Why he isn't here I don't know, but if you'll wait a few minutes—"

"Could I see anybody else in the meantime?"

"Well, there are two interesting men in the hospital. One is Lieut.-Commander Sandford, who was in charge of the submarine that blew up the viaduct—"

"I must see him at all costs!"

"I think I can arrange that. The other is Sergeant Finch, who's going to get the V.C. I'll telephone over to the hospital and let them know you're coming. Then I'll have Chater here by the time you get back."

Off I went to the hospital. Sergeant Finch, they told me, was downstairs, and Commander Sandford—he was Lieutenant Sandford when he went for the Mole—in a cubicle upstairs.

The sister in charge of Finch's ward met mc in the passage.

"I'm afraid you can't see Finch just at present."

"He is engaged, perhaps?"

"Yes, with the barber."

I peeped through the glass panel, and there, sure enough, was my hero with his face half-smothered in lather. So I climbed the stairs and was shown into Lieut.-Commander Sandford's tiny apartment.

"A friend to see you," announced the nurse.

"A stranger at present," I corrected her, "but not for long, I hope."

Lieut.-Commander Sandford seemed pleased to see me. I gathered that he was dull. It was a hard thing, I reflected, to be dull after charging into the Mole. However, somebody, no doubt, will make that up to him by and by.

He was young, this hero, and of a merry temperament. Our interview developed into quite a jovial affair.

"Badly wounded?" I asked.

"Oh, not so very. My hand, as you see, and I got one through the thigh."

"You'll soon be out and about, the doctor tells me. In the meantime, you've made a horrid mess of that viaduct."

"Have I?" he chuckled.

"Don't you know? Well, I can give you the latest information. It's all gone to glory. The Huns arc creeping backwards and forwards on a single plank."

"That's good." He laughed again.

"What exactly happened? I gather that you perched your submarine in the very middle of the woodwork beneath the viaduct?"

"There was no woodwork, so far as I know. You see, the Huns had covered all that over with a sort of steel curtain, but they'd left a hole in this curtain for the tide to run through. You know about the silt and all that? Well, as soon as we saw that hole we made straight for it."

"Were you on deck?"

"Oh, yes. We were all on deck."

"But how was it you weren't swept off the deck by the steel curtain?"

"Why, don't you see, we rammed her in as far as the conning-tower, and then she stuck. All I had to do after that was to launch a boat, get the men into it, touch the button that fired the fuse, climb into the boat after the men, and get clear away before the explosion took place."

"Oh! That was all, was it?"

"Yes. Unluckily we fouled the propeller of the boat, and so two of us had to row. There were only two oars. I don't suppose," he added, with a specially deep chuckle, "any two men ever pulled so hard before."

"You knew what was going to happen in a minute?"

"Rather! I'd pressed the button!"

"They let you get right up to the Mole, I understand?"

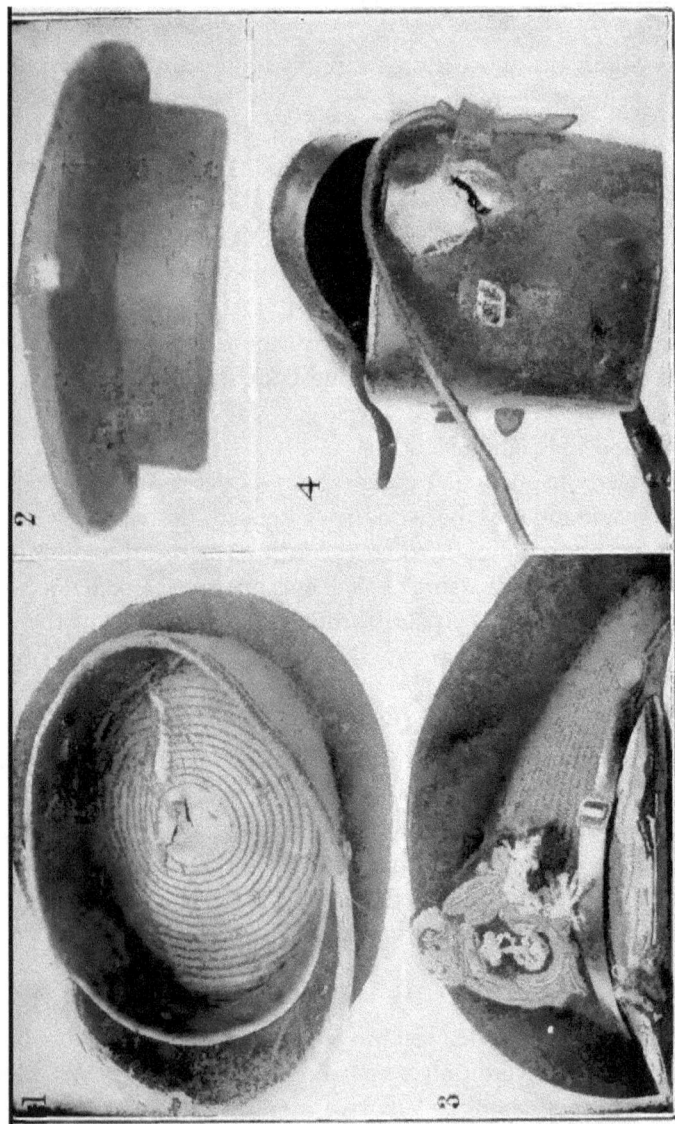

SOUVENIRS OF THE GREAT FIGHT: (1), (2) and (3) *Cap worn by Captain Carpenter during the Attack on Zeebrugge*; (4) *His Binocular Case pierced by Bullet or Shrapnel.*

"Yes. They all stopped firing. It was rather rum. I suppose they took it for granted we'd gone mad."

"They stood and watched you? I presume you know the actual viaduct was crowded with Huns?"

"No, I didn't. I'm glad I didn't."

"Why? Would you have felt some compunction in blowing them up?"

"Lord, no! But I was quite frightened enough as it was!"

We both laughed at that.

"Was it a good explosion?"

"I think so. I should have enjoyed it more, only just before it happened I got wounded."

"That was a pity. I was having a little chat with Captain Carpenter last night, and he tells me the flames were a mile high."

"A mile?" mused Mr. Sandford. "Golly! Some bang!"

"One of the best bangs on record," I assured him. "Now I must pop downstairs and see Sergeant Finch."

"Righto! I say, are you going to write about this stunt?"

"If I'm spared."

"Shall we have a chance of seeing it?"

"You shall," I promised him, and left him contentedly chuckling.

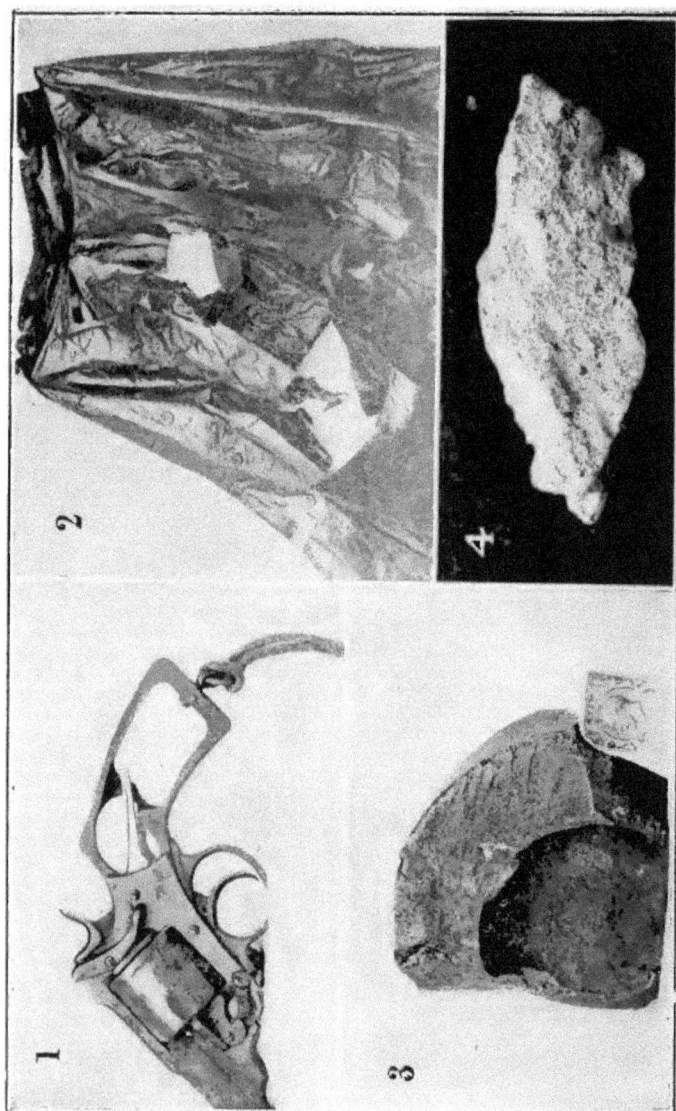

SOUVENIRS OF THE GREAT FIGHT: (1) Captain Carpenter's Revolver; (2) His Oilskin; (3) Piece of the German Shell which shattered the "Vindictive's" Chart-house; (4) Fragment of Zeebrugge Mole blown on board the

CHAPTER 8

What the Marines Told the Huns

Sergeant Finch, V.C, had finished his shave, and looked as clean and neat as any hero out of a fighting-top could expect.

"They tell me," I began, "that you've got the V.C. Congratulations!"

"Thank you, sir. But I don't know what I did to get it, and that's a fact. Seems to me if *one* has the V.C, the whole lot ought to have it."

"Still, that being impossible, they've made you the victim. How's the hand?"

"Going on a treat. I didn't want to come here. I wanted to go back to barracks with my pal. I never noticed I was hurt."

"Pretty hot in that fighting-top, wasn't it?"

"Pretty fair."

"I saw it this morning."

"Oh, did you, sir?" He was more interested now. "Then you saw where the shell came through, I suppose? We all went down in a bunch, and I had a job to get out from underneath."

"And then you went on working the gun?"

"I suppose I did, but I don't really know what I did. One of my pals was badly hit, and I tried to get him down on deck. I know that. But it's a fact I don't really know what I did. All I do know is I'm dreading this business that's coming."

"Don't you worry about that," I reassured him. "You'll find Somebody very charming to you."

"Oh, it isn't that part," replied the Sergeant. "It's getting back to the barracks."

He had visions, I could see, of impetuous and quite strange ladies flinging their arms about his modest neck.

"I shall look out for the snapshots."

Finch shrugged his shoulders, and I left him anticipating the worst.

SOUVENIR OF THE GREAT FIGHT

The Shot-riddled Chart of the "Vindictive" as recovered from the wreck of the Chart-house.

Captain Chater, who had been the adjutant of the Fourth Battalion Royal Marines, was busy down at the stables, but he very kindly came along to the Mess and made sketches on a piece of blotting paper. He was about twenty-three years of age, and had the same healthy delight in every kind of bang as Lieutenant-Commander Sandford. I understood him to say that the two senior officers. Colonel B. N. Elliot, D.S.O., R.M.L.I., and Major A. A. Cordner, were both killed on the port side of the bridge of the *Vindictive* whilst that vessel was approaching the Mole, and within only a hundred yards of it. (He was standing with them at the time.) This catastrophe left Major B. G. Weller, D.S.C., in command of the battalion.

"The most awkward part of the business," Captain Chater explained, "was that sixteen-foot drop. One didn't know, you see, what might be below. Not that the men minded. They were simply grand! Yelled like mad all the time, and went for the Huns as though the whole thing was a football match. The marines are rather bucked about the show."

"We all know about the marines—including the enemy! How did you feel on the way over?"

"Oh, I didn't feel much. We'd had two previous shots, you know. One was getting used to it."

"Did it seem a long time that you were on the Mole?"

"No. Awfully short! We were quite surprised when the signal came for us to get back. Getting back was the worst part. We had scaling ladders and ropes, but the fire was very heavy, and the men wouldn't go without their pals. They insisted on taking everybody, living or dead. You can imagine that that took time."

"Anyway," I suggested, "seeing that it's all over, what about hopping into the car with me and coming back to X——?"

For the first time during our conversation he grew serious.

"To tell you the truth," he admitted, in a low tone, "I've been racking my brains for an excuse to do that, and can't think of one!"

CHAPTER 9

I Hear They Want More

Two very brief conversations, and this imperfect and unpretentious chronicle of Zeebrugge comes to a close.

The first is with Commander E. O. B. Seymour Osborne, who had charge of the gunnery operations aboard the *Vindictive*. I found him at lunch with another officer in a pleasant apartment on the seafront at X——.

"I was told," I began, "that I must not leave without seeing you."

"Oh? I don't quite know why."

"You were in it, weren't you?"

"Yes, I was in it."

"And well in it, I believe?"

"Pretty well in it. Have a glass of port?"

"No, thanks."

"It will do you a lot of good."

"If you really think that——. Now, please tell me something."

"I'll tell you one thing. The men were great. I saw one chap come staggering on board with a pal in his arms. Whether the pal was alive or dead I couldn't say, and I doubt whether he could. But I heard him murmuring to him, 'I wouldn't leave yer, Bill ! Did you think I would?'"

That's all. The other remark, which has since proved highly significant, came from an officer who very courteously gave me a lift to the station in his car. No less a personage than the admiral came out to see him off.

'The admiral tells me," he observed, as we drove away, "that the standard was very high in this affair."

I made no comment. None was needed.

"By the way," he went on, "have you noticed that a lot of the chaps

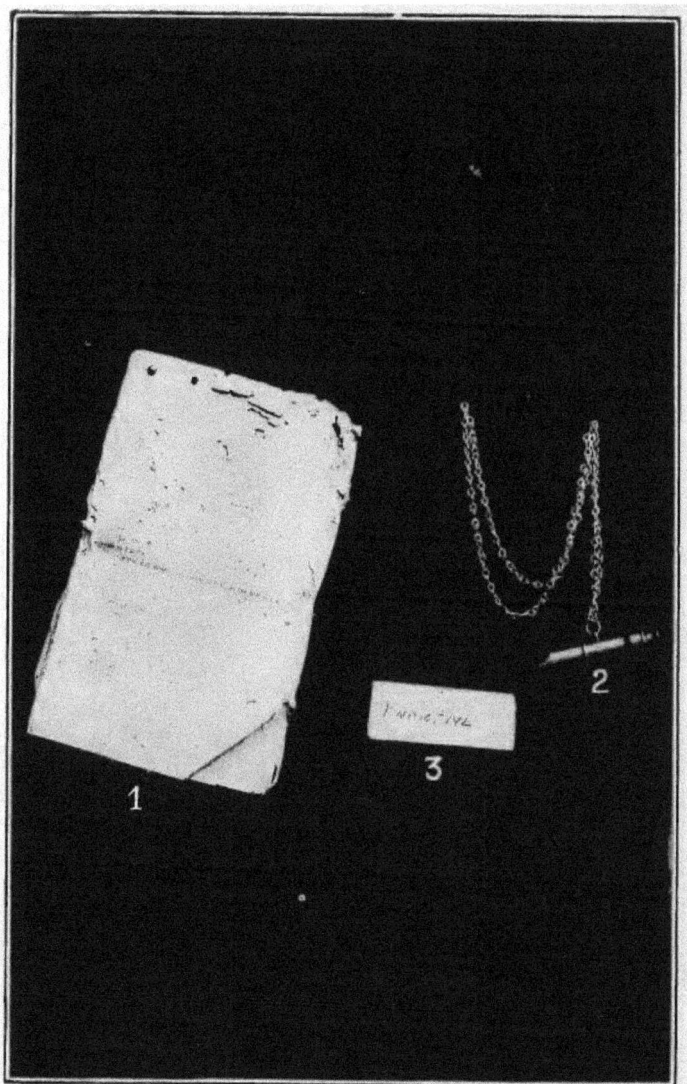

SOUVENIRS OF THE GREAT FIGHT: (1) *"Vindictive's" Operation Orders as Recovered from the Wrecked Chart-house;* (2) *Whistle blown as a Signal to Storm the Mole;* (3) *Token to be given to the Chief Engineer of the "Vindictive" to Scuttle the Ship if she became Disabled.*

seem a bit used up? Rather nervy and all that?"

"Not surprising, is it?"

"Well, it looks to me as though they want more of it."

They got it.

★★★★★

A thrill ran through England when it heard that the *Vindictive* had been sunk in the very jaws of Ostend Harbour. The imagination dwelt on the old battleship—scarred, battered, broken, covered with glory. They wanted to make a show of her, and a fine show she would have made; but her work was not jet done. One final honour was in store for her. Just as so many gallant men had died on her decks for the Cause of Freedom, so she, too, could perish in the same cause.